THE CHURCH AND THE WORLD

Gaudium et Spes, Inter Mirifica

REDISCOVERING VATICAN II

Rediscovering Vatican II is an eight-book series in commemoration of the fortieth anniversary of Vatican II. These books place the council in dialogue with today's church and are not just historical expositions. They answer the question: What do today's Catholics need to know?

This series will appeal to readers who have heard much about Vatican II, but who have never sat down to understand certain aspects of the council. Its main objectives are to educate people as to the origins and developments of Vatican II's key documents as well as to introduce them to the documents' major points; to review how the church (at large and in its many parts) since the council's conclusion has accepted and/or rejected and/or revised the documents' points in practical terms; and to take stock of the council's reforms and paradigm shifts, as well as of the directions that the church appears to be heading.

The completed series will comprise these titles:

Ecumenism and Interreligious Dialogue: Unitatis Redintegratio, Nostra Aetate by Cardinal Edward Cassidy

The Church and the World: Gaudium et Spes, Inter Mirifica by Norman Tanner

The Laity and Christian Education: Apostolicam Actuositatem, Gravissimum Educationis by Dolores Leckey

Liturgy: Sacrosanctum Concilium by Rita Ferrone

Scripture: Dei Verbum by Ronald Witherup

The Nature of the Church: Lumen Gentium, Christus Dominus, Orientalium Ecclesiarum by Richard Gaillardetz

Evangelization and Religious Freedom: Ad Gentes, Dignitatis Humanae by Thomas Stransky

Religious Life and Priesthood: Perfectae Caritatis, Optatam Totius, Presbyterorum Ordinis by Maryanne Confoy

The Church and the World

Gaudium et Spes, Inter Mirifica

Norman Tanner

Paulist Press
New York/Mahwah, NJ

Cover design by Amy King
Book design by Céline M. Allen

Copyright © 2005 by The Trustees for Roman Catholic Purpose

Cum permissu Superiorum
P. Francisco Egaña, SJ, Censor Deputatus

Library of Congress Cataloging-in-Publication Data

Tanner, Norman P.
   The church and the world : Gaudium et spes, Inter mirifica / Norman Tanner.
      p. cm. — (Rediscovering Vatican II)
   Includes bibliographical references and index.
   ISBN 0-8091-4238-4 (alk. paper)
   1. Vatican Council (2nd : 1962–1965). Constitutio pastoralis de ecclesia in mundo huius. 2. Church and the world. 3. Vatican Council (2nd : 1962–1965). Decretum de instrumentis communicationis socialis. 4. Mass media—Religious aspects—Catholic Church. 5. Catholic Church—Doctrines. I. Title. II. Series.
   BX8301962.A45 C9868 2005
   261—dc22
                                                        2005009270

Published by Paulist Press
997 Macarthur Boulevard
Mahwah, New Jersey 07430

www.paulistpress.com

Printed and bound in the
United States of America

CONTENTS

Acknowledgments vii

Abbreviations and Glossary ix

Introduction xi

SECTION I
PASTORAL CONSTITUTION ON THE CHURCH IN THE WORLD OF TODAY
Gaudium et Spes

Part I: The Document 3

Part II: Major Points 38

Part III: Implementation 61

Part IV: The State of the Questions 87

SECTION II
DECREE ON MEANS OF SOCIAL COMMUNICATION
Inter Mirifica

Part I: The Document 93

Part II: Major Points 104

Part III: Implementation 110

Part IV: The State of the Questions 116

NOTES 119

Part V: Further Reading...123

INDEX 127

ACKNOWLEDGMENTS

I thank Paulist Press for inviting me to write this book. My special thanks are due to Christopher Bellitto, editor of the series "Rediscovering Vatican II," who has provided much help and encouragement.

My interest in *Gaudium et Spes* came principally through being invited by Professor Giuseppe Alberigo, director of the "Istituto per le scienze religiose Giovanni XXIIII," Bologna, to write a chapter on the evolution of the decree at Vatican II for the history of the council that he edited (see below, p. 120, note 8). I thank him and those at the Institute who gave me support and hospitality: Alberto Melloni, Daniele Menozzi, Giuseppe Ruggieri, Giovanni Turbanti, Riccardo Burigana, Maria Teresa Fattori, Massimo Faggioli, and others.

Quotations from the two decrees, *Gaudium et Spes* and *Inter Mirifica*, are taken, with occasional modifications, from *Decrees of the Ecumenical Councils*, ed. Norman Tanner (Georgetown: Georgetown University Press, 1990), vol. 2. They are reprinted with kind permission from Georgetown University Press.

I thank the Jesuit community of the Gregorian University in Rome, my new home, for providing friendship and a suitable environment for the writing the book; and the community of Campion Hall, Oxford, my previous home for many years, for hospitality during the summer of 2004 when a part of the book was written.

Finally, I express my thanks to all those—my parents, family, friends, educators, and colleagues—who have helped me to appreciate Vatican II.

Norman Tanner, SJ
Gregorian University, Rome
February 26, 2005

ABBREVIATIONS AND GLOSSARY

Documents of Vatican II

AA	*Apostolicam Actuositatem* (Apostolate of the Laity)
AG	*Ad Gentes* (Missionary Activity)
CD	*Christus Dominus* (Bishops)
DH	*Dignitatis Humanae* (Religious Freedom)
DV	*Dei Verbum* (Revelation)
GE	*Gravissimum Educationis* (Christian Education)
GS	*Gaudium et Spes* (The Church in the World of Today)
IM	*Inter Mirifica* (Means of Social Communication/Mass Media)
LG	*Lumen Gentium* (The Church)
NA	*Nostra Aetate* (Non-Christian Religions)
OE	*Orientalium Ecclesiarum* (Eastern Catholic Churches)
OT	*Optatam Totius* (Priestly Formation)
PC	*Perfectae Caritatis* (Religious Life)
PO	*Presbyterorum Ordinis* (Ministry and Life of Priests)
SC	*Sacrosanctum Concilium* (Liturgy)
UR	*Unitatis Redintegratio* (Ecumenism)

Books

ADA

Acta et Documenta Concilio Oecumenico Vaticano II Apparando, series 1, *Antepraeparatoria* (Vatican City: Typis Polyglottis Vaticanis, 1960–69)

Alberigo, *Vatican II*

G. Alberigo and J. Komonchak, eds., *History of Vatican II* (Maryknoll, NY: Orbis/Leuven: Peeters, 1995–), 4 vols. so far. For the fifth (and last) volume, not yet published in English, references are to the Italian edition, *Storia del concilio Vaticano II*, ed. G. Alberigo (Bologna: Il Mulino, 1995–2001), vol. 5.

AS

Acta Synodalia Sacrosancti Concilii Oecumenici Vaticani II, 4 vols. (Vatican City: Typis Polyglottis Vaticanis, 1970–80)

Decrees   Norman Tanner, ed., *Decrees of the Ecumenical Coun-
                       cils*, 2 vols. (London: Sheed & Ward, subsequently
                       Continuum/Washington, DC: Georgetown Univer-
                       sity Press, 1990)

Latourelle, *Vatican II*   René Latourelle, *Vatican II: Assessment and Perspectives
                       Twenty-Five Years After (1962–1987)*, 3 vols. (New
                       York/Mahwah, NJ: Paulist Press, 1988–89)

Turbanti, *GS*   Giovanni Turbanti, *Un concilio per il mondo moderno:
                       La redazione della costituzione pastorale 'Gaudium et
                       spes' del Vaticano II* (Bologna: Il Mulino, 2000)

Other Abbreviations

A and B   Conservatives/Traditionalists and Progressives/Liberals (see p.
          119, note 3)

CLA   Commission for the Lay Apostolate (see p. 5)

CM   *Commissio mista*/Mixed commission (see p. 7)

DC   Doctrinal Commission (see p. 5)

PCSC   Pontifical Council of Social Communication (see p. 114)

SPMS   Secretariat for the Press and the Moderation of Shows (see p. 93)

Glossary

aula: the "hall" in which the debates were held, i.e., the nave of St. Peter's
          basilica (see p. 6)

decree/constitution/declaration: the various types of documents of the coun-
          cil (see footnote on p. xi)

"fathers": full members of the council, mainly bishops (see p. 120, note 6)

periti: those who attended the council as theological "experts" (see p. 120,
          note 6)

schema/schemata: draft decree(s) (see p. 4)

Schema XIII/Schema XVII: the names by which *Gaudium et Spes* was long
          known (see pp. 7 and 9)

votum/vota: response(s) submitted to Rome by bishops and others before the
          council began (see p. 3). For *Votum* as a document of the council,
          see p. 51.

INTRODUCTION

There are both contrasts and similarities between *Gaudium et Spes* and *Inter Mirifica*, the two decrees* of Vatican II that are the focus of this short book.

Inter Mirifica was among the first decrees to reach a conclusion. It and *Sacrosanctum Concilium* were definitively approved by the council and promulgated by Pope Paul VI on December 4, 1963, and so became the only two decrees to be approved by the end of the council's second period. *Gaudium et Spes* was the last of the sixteen decrees to be approved and promulgated, on December 7, 1965, the penultimate day of the council.

Inter Mirifica was among the least discussed decrees during the council. Only two and a half days were devoted to the formal debate on it. *Gaudium et Spes*, on the other hand, was the decree that received most attention after *Lumen Gentium*. The debate on it dominated proceedings during much of the third period of the council in the autumn of 1964 and it received further attention during the following year. *Inter Mirifica* is the shortest of the council's decrees except for *Nostra Aetate* and it has the middle status of a "decree"; *Gaudium et Spes* is the longest of all and has the most solemn status, that of a "constitution."

In terms of reception, *Gaudium et Spes* has been one of the most discussed of all the council's documents and has generally received a favorable reception both inside and beyond the Catholic Church. It has, moreover, had a considerable and direct influence upon developments

---

*The sixteen documents promulgated by the council are called, generically, "decrees." These "decrees" were divided, according to a descending gradation of authority, into four "constitutions" (*SC, LG, DV,* and *GS*), nine "decrees," and three "declarations." "Decree," therefore, has two meanings, a generic and a more specific one. *Gaudium et Spes* is one of the four most solemn documents, a "constitution"; *Inter Mirifica* has the status of a "decree."

xi

that have taken place both within the Catholic community and more widely. The reception of *Inter Mirifica*, in contrast, has been subdued and to a considerable extent negative, though the document, it will be argued, has been, even through its limitations, a stimulus to further reflection and action.

On the other hand, there are some basic and interesting similarities, which make it right that the two documents should find their way together into this volume. In terms of the council's organization, both decrees were the responsibility of the Commission for the Lay Apostolate, wholly so in the case of *Inter Mirifica*, and in conjunction with the Doctrinal Commission in the case of *Gaudium et Spes*. Both decrees made an interesting marriage of papal and conciliar teaching. That is to say, most of the material in *Inter Mirifica* and important parts of *Gaudium et Spes* had been treated extensively in papal encyclicals of the preceding half-century or so. As a result, the council could, and did, build on this earlier material.

Both decrees, moreover, treated of issues that were in tune with the lives of many people. The issues have retained their relevance, indeed grown therein, during the forty years since the end of the council. This looks set to continue into the foreseeable future. *Gaudium et Spes* was unequalled among the council's decrees in its outward-going nature, both in the kind of material it dealt with and in the fact that it alone explicitly addressed itself beyond the Christian community to all people of good will. *Inter Mirifica* was less successful in this respect in terms of format, yet in terms of subject matter, the influence of the mass media upon the thinking and outlook of society at large is greater today than ever before.

SECTION I
PASTORAL CONSTITUTION ON
THE CHURCH IN THE WORLD OF TODAY

Gaudium et Spes

PART I

THE DOCUMENT

PREPARATION

Gaudium et Spes emerged only gradually from the womb of the council.

Right from the beginning, Pope John XXIII had indicated that he wanted the council to be pastoral. Thus when on January 25, 1959, a mere three months after his election as pope, in the course of a short address to a group of cardinals gathered "in consistory" in the Church of St. Paul Outside the Walls in Rome, he first publicly announced his intention to call an ecumenical council, he said its purpose would be "to come to grips with the spiritual needs of the present time." Some two years later, in the bull *Humanae Salutis* of December 25, 1961, by which the pope formally convoked the council, he explained further what he meant by these spiritual needs. His words were as follows:

> In the presence of this twofold spectacle—a world revealing a serious state of spiritual need and the church of Christ, still so vibrant with life—we have felt at once, right from the time of our election as pope, the urgent duty to call together our sons in order to enable the church to contribute more effectively towards solving the problems of the modern age.

During the preparation for the council, which lasted almost four years, from the initial announcement in January 1959 to the start of the council in October 1962, two important processes took place. First, all the bishops of the world as well as various other individuals and some institutions, such as Catholic universities, were invited to send to Rome their views on what they hoped from the forthcoming council. The responses, submitted in writing, were called *vota* (singular, *votum*).

Second, ten preparatory commissions and several "secretariats" were established by the pope with the responsibility of preparing draft decrees that would be put before the council and would take into account the views expressed in the *vota*. The preparatory commissions and secretariats, which were largely controlled by the Roman Curia,[1] had ready, or (as in most cases) in preparation, seventy draft decrees (called *schema*, plural *schemata*) by the time the council met in October 1962.

Neither the *vota* nor the draft decrees, both of which can be read in full (almost all in Latin, following the regulations then in force) in the published *Acta* of the council,[2] showed much anticipation of the eventual format of *Gaudium et Spes*.

Altogether some 2,150 out of the 2,812 individuals and groups who were invited to submit a *votum* did so. As would be expected, this large number of responses revealed a fair range of opinions. Nevertheless, they show relatively little of the openness toward the world of the time that was eventually to prove one of the most notably features of *Gaudium et Spes*. On the one hand, the responses of those who emerged as the conservative minority (hereafter called A) in the council showed plenty of concern for the contemporary world, but their approach was largely to lament or condemn recent developments, such as the rise of Communism or the loss of the church's influence in political and social affairs. On the other hand, the replies of many of those who emerged as the progressive majority (hereafter called B) saw reform of the church as the key, so the dynamic advocated was that a reformed church would be better able to confront the contemporary world, rather than that the church (or the council, or Christians more generally) should listen to what the world of the time (including the non-Catholic and non-Christian world) was saying and doing, whether for good or for evil.[3] A notable and often quoted case of apparent unawareness is the *votum* of Denis Hurley, archbishop of Durban in South Africa. He had already established himself as a noted opponent of *apartheid* and was to emerge as a leading B in the council and proponent of *Gaudium et Spes*. Yet he did not raise the issue of racial discrimination in his extensive *votum*.[4]

The seventy draft decrees largely followed the A line. This is to be expected, inasmuch as the preparation of them was largely in the hands of the curia, as mentioned. But an additional reason was the division of competence within the preparatory commissions and secretariats: namely, between doctrinal or theological issues on the one hand, and those of a pastoral or disciplinary nature on the other hand. That is to say, it was decided that all issues touching theology/doctrine were to be dealt with by one of the ten preparatory commissions, the "Doctrinal Commission" (= DC). This commission was dominated by—indeed was almost an extension of—the Holy Office, the congregation in the Roman curia responsible for doctrinal orthodoxy. The formidable Cardinal Ottaviani was both working head of the Holy Office (formally he was number two, the "secretary," since the pope was the prefect) and prefect of the DC. The Holy Office, and as a result the DC, especially in the early stages of the council, was a notably strong supporter of the A approach. Issues of a pastoral and disciplinary nature were then divided among the other preparatory commissions and secretariats. But "pastoral issues" tended to mean little more than practices and techniques, since theological concerns were, in theory, excluded. For these nine commissions, the result was that any serious dialogue with the modern world, including its non-Catholic and secular intelligentsia, was almost impossible inasmuch as consideration of theological aspects was essential if the dialogue was to be conducted in any depth and yet such consideration was excluded from their competence.

In fact, however, the situation was more propitious. While it is true that there was little anticipation of the eventual format and approach of *Gaudium et Spes*, nevertheless almost all the individual issues eventually discussed in the document had been raised, one way or another, in the *vota* and the draft decrees. In the case of the *vota*, it is necessary to search through them in the published *Acta*, since relevant points appear here and there, often unexpectedly.[5] Regarding the draft decrees, of the seven presented by the DC to Pope John shortly before the beginning of the council, four dealt with various issues that would be treated in *Gaudium et Spes*, namely those entitled *De Ordine Morali* (The Moral Order), *De Castitate, Matrimonio, Familia, Virginitate* (Chastity, Marriage, the Family, and Virginity), *De Ordine Sociali* (The Social Order), *De Communitate Gentium* (The Community of Nations). The decrees being prepared by another of the preparatory commissions, the Commission for the Lay Apostolate (= CLA), also touched on issues that would appear in *Gaudium et Spes*.

Influential, too, was Pope John's encyclical on Catholic social teaching, *Mater et Magistra*, which was promulgated in May 1961, the seventieth anniversary of Pope Leo XIII's social encyclical, *Rerum Novarum*. While *Mater et Magistra* repeated many traditional formulations, it introduced new ideas and approaches. Its method was more inductive than deductive, taking as its starting point concrete and current issues rather than a code of somewhat abstract principles. It spoke about many social and economic issues that would be treated in *Gaudium et Spes*, including some that were especially relevant to the so-called third world, such as colonialism and economic development. It would be going too far to describe the encyclical as a blueprint for *Gaudium et Spes*; nevertheless it anticipated much of the eventual approach and content of the decree and showed in the clearest terms the pope's commitment to the issues at stake.

FIRST AND SECOND PERIODS AND THE INTERSESSIONS, 1962–64

The first period of the council lasted from October 11 to December 8, 1962. During this time the members of the council[6] normally met for official business each weekday morning in Rome's most famous church, St. Peter's basilica ("basilica" = large church) in the Vatican City. The debates, and other official business conducted in the basilica, were referred to as the proceedings in the *aula* (that is, the "hall" or council chamber). The great drama of the two months was the rejection by the large majority of the council of the seventy decrees that had been drafted by the preparatory commissions and secretariats. The rejection was radical. It was made clear that the draft decrees were fundamentally inadequate, that they could not be improved upon to the satisfaction of the majority in the council, and that as a result they would have to be withdrawn and the council would more or less have to start afresh. This amounted to quite a revolution. Indeed it constituted the first time in the history of the church that the expected agenda of an ecumenical council had been so thoroughly overturned.

In hindsight it is possible to see more continuity. That is to say, as mentioned earlier, many of the issues covered by the sixteen decrees that were eventually to be approved by the council can be found in the seventy preparatory decrees. But in format and approach there would be radical changes. The revolution began with the rejection of the preparatory decrees on revelation and the church. By the end of the first session it was clear that the mostly short decrees on various topics that eventually found their way into *Gaudium et Spes* would also have to be abandoned.

Painful as the process was, one has to admire the speed with which the council came to terms with the collapse of the prepared agenda. In early December 1962, when the need for a second period of the council became evident, the number of decrees that would be debated at it was reduced from the original seventy to twenty, and then in January 1963, after the end of the first period, to seventeen. The last of these seventeen, and hence known for a long time as "Schema XVII," was entitled "The Presence of the Church in the Modern World." This was the decree that eventually developed into *Gaudium et Spes*—"eventually" because of all Vatican II's decrees, *Gaudium et Spes* had the longest and most tortuous evolution.

Some initial work was done on Schema XVII in the first "intersession." This was the time between the end of the first period of the council in December 1962 and the beginning of the second in October 1963, a period during which most of the bishops were back in their dioceses and the members of the conciliar commissions[7]—who included both bishops and other "fathers" of the council and theologians/*periti*—undertook the work of drafting the new decrees, each commission meeting together from time to time for this purpose. Responsibility for Schema XVII was entrusted to a commission drawn from members of both the DC and the CLA.

This "mixed commission"—*Commissio mista* as it was officially called (= CM)—made some headway during the intersession in drawing up a draft decree. Not surprisingly, however, in view of the large numbers of issues that had to be covered and the fact that the commission was starting almost from scratch, satisfaction with the work was far from complete. Matters were compounded by the introduction of a parallel draft, known as the "Malines text" (Cardinal Suenens, archbishop of Malines in Belgium, was the main architect, assisted by other Belgian bishops and theologians; their meetings were usually held in Malines). The authorization that was alleged to have been given by the council for this alternative text was much disputed.

A further contribution was Pope John XXIII's last encyclical, *Pacem in Terris*, which was published in April 1963, less than two months before his death. It urged peace among nations, based upon truth, justice, charity, and freedom, and the right organization of society. It was addressed to all people of good will, not just to Catholics, and included a plea for the ending of the arms race, a ban on nuclear weapons, and eventual disarmament. The threat to peace and the possibility of a nuclear catastrophe had been brought to the forefront of world attention in October 1962, during the first period of the council, when the two superpowers, the United States and the Soviet Union, came close to war over nuclear missiles supplied by the latter to Cuba. The continuing urgency of the world situation, the widespread appreciation of the encyclical's teachings, together with John XXIII's own prestige and popularity, which grew with the worldwide outpouring of grief at his final illness and death in June 1963, all added to the authority of the encyclical and it in turn—like *Mater et Magistra*—much influenced the eventual contents and style of *Gaudium et Spes*.

During the second period of the council, from September 19 to December 4, 1963, when once again all the members of the council gathered in Rome, little further progress was made on the decree. The eleven weeks were dominated by debates on various other decrees, principally *Lumen Gentium*. Indeed the council authorities had already decided in August 1963 that discussion of Schema XVII would probably not form part of the agenda of the forthcoming session. There was the vast and seemingly intractable nature of the material and the unresolved issue of the Malines text's status. There was also tension within the CM, principally between members who belonged to the DC and those who belonged to the CLA. The latter resented the DC's claim that all issues of a theological nature belonged exclusively to its competence. Paul VI, moreover, had succeeded John XXIII and his interest lay more with *Lumen Gentium* than with *Gaudium et Spes*. It was only in November 1963, when it was already clear that a third session would be necessary, that the council began to wake up to the stalled fate of Schema XVII. There had still been no formal debate on the decree, only a brief report on the progress (or lack of it) so far made, which was given to the council fathers on December 2.

During the following intersession, however, the work of the CM was intense. Much of it was done by sub-groups of the CM meeting in various locations around Europe. Altogether the document went through a dozen revisions during a ten-month period. Its official title was changed first to "The Active Participation of the Church in the Building of the World" and then to its final title, "The Church in the World of Today" *(De Ecclesia in Mundo Huius Temporis)*. The working title by which it continued to be known changed to "Schema XIII" (following a reordering of the proposed decrees). Some of the better-known phrases and characteristics of the final version also emerged, such as the opening words of the document—"The joy and sorrows, the hopes and anxieties of the people of our time"—and the attention to "signs of the times."

There was tension within the CM between those who wanted a theological approach and those who wanted to begin, rather, with the world and humanity, a more sociological approach. The conflict cut across A and B lines somewhat. Thus, B theologians were divided on the issue, including the two who were probably the most influential among them. Karl Rahner, the German Jesuit, urged a more strictly theological approach and remained critical, almost contemptuous, of the decree right through to the end on account of its empirical nature, while the French Dominican Yves Congar was glad of the decree's readiness to address concrete issues. To some extent this was reflected in the generally different approaches of German and French theologians.

Also involved was the issue of whether it was right in principle for an ecumenical council to speak about gray areas of human existence, which involved the contingencies of economics, politics, and social conditions, or whether rather it should confine itself to theological principles of a more certain and lasting value. For some—perhaps concentrating too much on Trent and Vatican I and forgetting the contingency and particularity of many disciplinary decrees of the early and medieval councils—this adventure into the details of human life seemed unprecedented for an ecumenical council and beneath its dignity. In a similar vein, Karl Rahner and Gerard Philips, the influential Belgian theologian, criticized the various drafts of *Gaudium et Spes* for failing to distinguish properly between the natural and supernatural orders. There was also the question of whether the decree was indulging in superficial humanism and naive optimism about the human state and being insufficiently attentive to evil and the reality of sin. Some theologians, moreover, who might appear to be of a predominantly A mold, such as Monsignor Pavan, professor of the Lateran University in Rome and one of the principal architects of Pope John's encyclicals *Mater et Magistra* and *Pacem in Terris*, were happy, at least in principle, with the more "from below" approach. It was the latter, identified with French theologians, that prevailed.

A further twist was given toward the end of the intersession when Karol Wojtyła, Archbishop of Cracow, submitted an alternative schema on behalf of the Polish bishops. It emphasized, especially, the rights of the church to exercise its ministry and the rights of Christians to practice their religion. The commission declined to accept this document as the basis for its work, mainly because it preferred to remain with its own drafts and to avoid ambiguities similar to those that had befallen the Malines text; perhaps too because the contents seemed too dependent upon the particular circumstances then prevailing in Communist Poland. Nevertheless, it was kept on hold and exerted some influence upon the further revisions of the decree in the summer of 1965.

THIRD PERIOD, AUTUMN 1964[8]

Gaudium et Spes became the centerpiece of the council's third period, which lasted from September 14 to November 21, 1964. The final version of the text that had been composed during the previous intersession, with its new title, "The Church in the World of Today," was sent by the CM to all the members of the council in July, together with a request that they submit their comments to the commission. From the start of the period it was expected that *Gaudium et Spes* would occupy a central place in the agenda, though in fact it was not until October 20 that the debate in the *aula* began.

In the meantime, indeed, the very existence of *Gaudium et Spes* as a decree of the council appeared to be threatened. Opposition came from various quarters. There was dislike of and tension over the contents of the decree, as mentioned above; there was also a feeling that discussion of it would take up so much time that it would be impossible to conclude the council during the third period, as many hoped—indeed, that as a result the council might drift on indefinitely and out of control. There was some concern about the way the July text had been composed, and so doubts about its regularity arose, in particular relating to whether the DC had been adequately consulted. The opposition was supported, even led, by the secretary-general of the council, Archbishop Felici, who had much influence over the council's agenda.

This hostility, somewhat behind the scenes, seems to have reinforced the determination of the large majority of the council that proper time be given to discussion of the document and in this way expectations were heightened. The wishes of the majority were expressed strongly in the influential meetings of the delegates of episcopal conferences (of regions, countries, or groups of countries) that took place fairly regularly in this third period. Monsignor Roger Etchegaray (later Cardinal Archbishop of Marseilles, France), who acted as secretary to these semi-official gatherings, summarized the mood, in his notes, as follows:

> Schema XIII is of the greatest importance, is the common opinion of the delegates after having consulted their conferences (9 October). We desire that Schema XIII, which the public opinion of many countries awaits eagerly, should play a role of capital importance in the pastoral work undertaken by the church. It corresponds to one of the major objectives given to the council by your Holiness and Pope John XXIII and, in searching for God's invitation in the signs of the times, it presents itself to us as a happy complement to the schema *De ecclesia*. In our opinion it would therefore be appropriate to take every means to give the schema the position that its subject-matter requires (letter to Pope Paul VI signed by twenty-three episcopal conferences, 11 or 12 October). Importance of the schema: very great on the pastoral level; very great on the ecumenical level; complement of *De ecclesia*; synthesis of all the schemata (15 October).

The debate in the *aula* finally got under way on October 20. The text of the schema was that sent out to the members of the council in July, though their subsequent comments were taken into consideration

in the brief "Directions for the future revision of the text" which the
CM had issued shortly after the beginning of the third period. The
structure of the schema was as follows:

Introduction
Chapter 1: Integral Vocation of the Human Person
Chapter 2: The Church in the Service of God and Humanity
Chapter 3: Conduct of Christians in the World
Chapter 4: Chief Responsibilities of Christians Today
Conclusion

Discussion of the text dominated the council proceedings for the
next three weeks until November 10. It occupied all the time assigned
for debate in the *aula* during this time—that is, each weekday morning, from 9 AM to 1 PM —except for a short period in early November.
Altogether nearly two hundred speeches were made (the normal time-
limit being ten minutes); some fifty others were scheduled but time
prevented their being delivered; and two hundred or so written statements were submitted to the CM in the names of individuals or
groups. By any standards, the schema was given an exceptionally full
airing and it captured the imagination of the assembly.

The agenda was carefully structured. Four mornings were dedicated to the schema as a whole, then came discussion of the Introduction and each of the schema's four chapters. The debate is not
easy to summarize—as is to be expected in view of the number and
the diversity of backgrounds of the speakers and others present. There
were many crosscurrents and it is important to avoid superficial cat-
egorization.

Speeches had to be written out beforehand and handed into the
council authorities several days before they were delivered, as in the
debates on other decrees; moreover, they were written and delivered
in Latin. Inevitably the speeches of those unfamiliar with Latin were
somewhat stilted and there was a fair amount of repetition. There was
also development, as later speakers showed more awareness of earlier
speeches and through the skillful arrangement of the agenda.

The Schema as a Whole

Almost all the speakers seemed to accept the importance of what was being discussed. No longer was there significant opposition—open, at least—to a decree of this kind on the grounds of its unsuitability for an ecumenical council. Only a few were thoroughly negative. Cardinal Heenan, archbishop of Westminster in England, was one of them, interestingly so in view of the pastoral nature of the decree and the fact that he was noted for his attention to pastoral issues. He thought the schema, as it stood, was unworthy of an ecumenical council and had failed the hopes of everyone.

The dominant impression was favorable, of gratitude and praise that something serious had been attempted. There was consensus that the schema, however imperfect it might be, sought to speak about a subject that was of great significance and that it was very important for the council to issue a decree on the topic.

In many cases the praise was fulsome, especially in the opening days when the schema as a whole was debated. The impression is that leading B's, and others, were determined to orchestrate a strong initial defense of the decree, in order to preempt any possibility of the council abandoning it. Cardinal Cento, of the Roman Curia, who as co-president of the CM introduced the schema to the assembly—and who might have been expected, therefore, to strike a positive note— claimed that no other document of the council had aroused "such great and widespread expectations." He hoped that after it had been improved upon as a result of the points that would be raised in the debate, it might be offered to everyone: Christians, believers, and atheists. Cardinal Liénart, archbishop of Lille in France, the first speaker after Cento, said the schema "succeeded in providing...almost all the essential elements of the help that the church can and ought to offer to the world"; Cardinal Spellman of New York thought it carried the "fundamental hope" of the council and that it was "an excellent, clear and sincere affirmation of how the church sees its role at the present time." From Germany, Cardinal Döpfner of Munich, who spoke in the name of eighty-three German and Scandinavian bishops, hoped the schema would be considered the "true crown" of the council; and Cardinal Bea, head of the Roman Curia's Secretariat for Christian

Unity, thought it "collected very difficult material in an excellent way and expounded succinctly the various parts." Karol Wojtyła, archbishop of Cracow in Poland, speaking in the name of the Polish episcopate, was also generous in his praise, even though, as mentioned, he had earlier submitted an alternative schema.

One frequent criticism was that the words *church* and *world* were used indiscriminately, without proper attention to their different meanings. "Church sometimes means the people of God, sometimes the ecclesiastical hierarchy, but the difference is not made clear," complained Cardinal Landazuri Ricketts, archbishop of Lima (Peru). He also wanted "world" to be defined. Others complained of insufficient clarity regarding the purpose of the schema. Was it meant to teach Christians how to live, or was it intended rather to enter into dialogue with non-Christians? Cardinal Morcillo of Madrid addressed the issue thus: "The schema appears to—indeed it should—address both Christians and non-Christians, believers and atheists. It is necessary, however, to use different language when speaking to Christians and non-Christians. Yet the schema uses the same language and arguments for both groups, for those who have faith in God and unbelievers."

Two other general concerns were, first, whether the right balance had been achieved between the vocation of people in this life and their eternal or eschatological calling, between the natural and the supernatural; second, whether there should be more concentration on the church's teaching or, rather, on "signs of the times." Both concerns reflected, in different ways, tension between "from above" and "from below" approaches.

Regarding the first concern, contrast Cardinal Liénart with Paul Meouchi, the Maronite patriarch of Antioch. The former spoke in tones redolent of post-war western Europe: "The natural order should be better distinguished from the supernatural....It is very important that in the schema we situate ourselves at once at the natural level and tell the world how we properly recognise the dignity of humankind, how we entirely approve of their legitimate ambitions, indeed we wish to be present to their work, in the realms of science and technology, inasmuch as these conform to God's intention, who gave to his rational creatures full government of this created world." The latter spoke in a more cautious Eastern voice: "The church's mission is described exclusively in terms of solving the temporal problems of this world, as if the church existed only to do works of charity, or to resolve social and economic problems among people. The divine purpose in establishing the church is not adequately propounded."

Regarding the second concern, various speakers wanted more emphasis upon the church's traditional teachings. Cardinal Heenan attacked the *periti* responsible for the schema (he seems to have had in mind especially Bernard Häring, the Redemptorist moral theologian, who was secretary of the sub-commission of the CM that had drafted the schema and who had clashed with Heenan earlier in the year in England on the issue of birth control). The *periti* were, he feared, being permitted to replace the ordinary magisterium of bishops and pope. Cardinal Ruffini wanted much more explicit reference to the social encyclicals of recent popes, especially Leo XIII, Pius XI, Pius XII, John XXIII, and Paul VI. Bishop Vairo of Gravina and Irsina, in Italy, pleaded for scholastic philosophy: "We wonder whether the church, in accommodating herself to the spirit of contemporary learning, which smacks of existentialism, historicism and pragmatism, is not renouncing, to the detriment of truth, the philosophy that has been proclaimed for centuries in catholic schools, that defends the pursuit of unchangeable truth and undisputed metaphysical principles, and whose fundamental affirmations have been traced by the church's magisterium to the source of divine revelation." On the other hand, Cardinal John Sheehan, archbishop of Baltimore (USA), proposed a much more dynamic concept of doctrine, praising the way the church had advanced in doctrine and structures and quoting John Henry Newman's remark in his *Essay on the Development of Christian Doctrine*, "a power of development is a proof of life."

Regarding "signs of the times," the comments varied considerably. Cardinal Léger of Montreal in Canada applauded the schema for discussing them but urged that they be viewed from a more evangelical perspective. A good number of bishops wanted a much fuller treatment of atheism and an explicit condemnation of Marxist Communism. Thus, Yü Pin, the exiled archbishop of Nanking in China, speaking in the name of more than seventy bishops, mostly from China and other countries of Asia, wanted the schema to contain a full chapter on atheistic Communism, which he described as the culmination of all heresies, so as to satisfy the expectations of all those who "groan under the yoke of Communism and endure unspeakable sufferings." Cardinal Suenens took a more conciliatory approach. Atheists, he said, should be engaged in dialogue in the hope that "they may seek and recognise the true image of God, which may be hidden under the caricatures they reject." In a similar vein, Cardinal Silva Henriquez, archbishop of Santiago in Chile, urged that condemnation was not enough: "The church must try to understand on what truth the error grows."

Many bishops, notably those belonging to the group called "Church of the Poor,"[9] urged, among "signs of the times," greater attention to poverty in the world. Lándazuri Ricketts spoke of the imbalance that exists in a world where two-thirds of the population own less than a fifth of the wealth. Hunger, especially, he said, needed more attention: "Of the fifty million people who die every year, thirty-five million die of hunger or insufficient food. In the name of Him who had pity on the crowd suffering from hunger, this assembly cannot avoid this problem.... We can and must exhort those people who have, to recognise their duty to satisfy those who have not." More radically, Bishop Soares de Resende of Beira (Mozambique) wanted "not just a church of the poor, but also a poor church," and he questioned the value of various church insignia—gold and bejewelled rings and pectoral crosses, colored *cappa-magnas*, and so on—and dignities that had not been instituted by Christ. Bishop Tchidimbo of Conakry (Guinea), suggested that lack of attention to poverty and other injustices was the main reason why the text appeared too Western in its outlook: "The schema has been conceived for Europe and perhaps for America, but not sufficiently for the Third World.... I find no mention in it of the difficulties of the peoples of Africa: underdevelopment, colonialism, discrimination according to race or colour, and no further description of the structures of a new society."

There were also requests for more input from the laity. Cardinal Léger was most outspoken: "Various experts, men and women, should explain the facts regarding hunger in the world, the family, peace, and so on. If our schema hopes to respond to today's issues, surely we must first hear how they are understood by those who live in the world." He urged, too, that laypeople be invited to speak in the *aula*. Archbishop Darmajuwana of Semarang (Indonesia) argued, even more strongly, that the laity should have the main role in discerning and resolving the issues.

Chapter 1: Our Vocation

After four packed and emotional days of debate on the schema as a whole, discussion turned to the first chapter, "Integral Vocation of the Human Person." Since this too was a vast and somewhat general topic, it is not surprising that the speeches contained a fair amount of repetition of what had already been said in the debate on the schema as a whole. Key contributions focused on the importance of taking the world seriously and the need for a better theological basis to the schema. Both issues revealed the varying A and B approaches. Emphasis upon taking the world seriously came mostly from bishops from northwestern Europe. Thus, Bishop Schmitt of Metz in France wanted more appreciation of the "novelty" of the modern world, which stands "in a certain dynamic solidarity with the progress and fortune of the gospel," so that if the church is to be missionary "it must enter into the historical progress of the world." Regarding a better theological basis, opinions varied: Bishop Garcia de Sierra y Mendez of Burgos (Spain) wanted the chapter to begin with the human person "as king of creation, over which God has granted him lordship." Another Spanish bishop, Romero Menjibar of Jaen, urged rather that the starting point be the church as the "community of salvation," intended by God to continue in history the "mystery of the incarnation and redemption." Abbot Prou, of the Benedictine monastery of Solesmes in France, wanted a clearer distinction between the natural and supernatural orders and more emphasis upon the role of grace in raising us to the supernatural level. Bishop Ziadé of Beirut (Lebanon) wanted a more theological and scriptural exposition of "signs of the times": they must be seen as "signs of the Lord's coming," not just "created things that manifest the Creator."

The boldest approach was struck by Bishop Tenhumbert, auxiliary of Münster (Germany). The church, he said, should acknowledge that in the past it had often been blind to the signs of the times or very slow to recognize them. Many men and women who discerned them correctly were for long rejected by the church: for example, founders of religious orders such as Ignatius of Loyola, Vincent de Paul, Francis de Sales, John de la Salle, and Mary Ward, together with many of their followers. To prevent this occurring again, various things would be needed: a renewed theology of the life and working of the Holy

Spirit in the church; a return to the model of authority in the church exercised by Christ, his apostles, and the Fathers, so as "not to extinguish the Spirit but to test all things and to hold on to what is good" (1 Thess 5:19–21); a new appreciation of the charisms and gifts of the people of God. Above all, a new style of authority in the church was necessary.

Chapters 2 and 3: Service of the Church and Conduct of Christians

Chapter 2, "The Church in the Service of God and Humanity," and chapter 3, "Conduct of Christians in the World," were debated together. Several speakers again emphasized the great importance of the schema as a whole: of more interest to the world than *De Ecclesia*, said Bishop Čule of Mostar (Yugoslavia); "of the utmost importance" and eventually to become, he hoped, the "crown" of the council, said Archbishop Golland Trindade of Botacatú (Brazil). Also stressed again was the importance of the church getting involved in temporal affairs, and the fact that this involvement formed an integral part of its mission. Dialogue with scientists was advocated. Various speakers wanted more treatment in the document of the types of involvement that are appropriate for the church. Today, said Cardinal Marty of Paris, the church no longer controls the world, as it did in the medieval West; so now it should act rather as a leaven in the world, "becoming incarnate in cultures that are very diverse." Cardinal Frings of Cologne struck a more cautious note. He thought chapter 3 put too much emphasis upon an incarnational theology: the incarnation, he argued, leads to the mysteries of the cross and resurrection and these need to be emphasized more.

Several speakers drew attention to the decadence of modern civilization. The Christian nations of the West produce far more obscene writings and visual material than do atheists in the East, argued Bishop Čule. Human beings today, led on by the advances of science, are making themselves into gods, thinking they are omniscient and omnipotent, observed Bishop Klepacz, auxiliary of Lodz (Poland). Pride, the root of sin, suffuses modern culture; what is needed is penitence, true metanoia, a turning toward God, which brings proper respect for creatures instead of an inordinate attachment to them, argued another Polish bishop, Zygfryd Kowalski, auxiliary of Chelmo. Among other topics that were aired anew or revisited were the importance of poverty, the need for dialogue with scientists, and a move away from legalism. Regarding the last, the outspoken Maximus IV Saigh, Melchite patriarch of Antioch, put it simply: the "legalist spirit," which has prevailed since the sixteenth century and which "blocks the energy of priests and faithful," must be consigned to the past; now, rather, the "law of grace and love" should reign.

Chapter 4: Responsibilities of Christians

Entitled, "Chief Responsibilities of Christians Today," this was the most detailed of the four chapters. It was first debated as a whole, briefly, and then its articles were debated individually. The headings and numbers of the articles were as follows:

Introduction (19)
Promoting the Dignity of the Person (20)
Marriage and the Family (21)
Culture (22)
Economic and Social Life (23)
Promoting Solidarity among the Family of Peoples (24)
Strengthening Peace (25)

Articles 20 to 25 roused much interest, notably among Asian and African bishops.

Article 20: Human Dignity

Regarding human dignity, there was general satisfaction that the chapter began with this consideration inasmuch as the human person is to be considered the starting point of both the opportunities and the problems of the contemporary world. Many speakers, however, wanted a better foundation, especially more attention to the God-given nature of this dignity, to the importance of our continuing relationship with God, and hence to the transcendent value of human life.

Bishop Athaide of Agra, a missionary in India, showed breadth of vision in praising Mahatma Gandhi and Vinobba Ghave, John Kennedy and Martin Luther King, as crusaders for social justice and better conditions of life, alongside innumerable Christians who had made heroic efforts of a similar kind. He was glad the schema encouraged Christians to work in these ways and to cooperate with others in their endeavors. Also from India, Duraisamy Lourdusamy, then an auxiliary bishop of Bangalore and later to become archbishop of the same city, speaking in the name of almost all the bishops from India, more than sixty of them, urged that giving material aid to people in need is not enough. Most important, he said, is "emotional integration, a sense of unity and equality among all people, whether rich or poor, prosperous or needy, healthy or sick, the highest or lowest in society. That is, psychological help is required more than physical and material, help that comes from and goes to the heart."

Three other issues received attention. Bishop De la Chanonie of Clermont (France) wanted the schema to speak about young people who are handicapped, whether physically, psychologically, or mentally. More was required of the church, he said, to help such people, who are numerous, indeed one in four young people in France, to fulfill their human calling in both the natural and the supernatural order. Second, several speakers urged that the schema speak more clearly against the evils of racial and other forms of discrimination. Archbishop Malula of Leopoldville (Congo) wanted the council to include in its condemnation of racism a form of it that he regarded as especially prevalent in Africa, namely "tribalism, whose poison not even Christians avoid, and which carries with it the fruits of death: hatred, fear, violence, revenge and slaughter." The third issue was women. Malula also spoke about this issue in Africa, where, he acknowledged, women are far from equal to men. He hoped the church would work toward "the promotion of woman to her full dignity and responsibility" and would set a good example by giving women a greater role within the church. Bishop Coderre of Saint-Jean de Québec (Canada), speaking in the name of forty bishops mainly from Canada, applauded the recent evolution in the consciousness of women regarding their dignity, which he considered to be in accordance with scripture and which he urged the church to "proclaim and promote."

Article 21: Marriage and the Family

Discussion of article 21, on marriage and the family, was strongly influenced by the fact that the council authorities—first Bishop Guano, president of the sub-commission of the CM responsible for drafting the schema, in his October 23 speech concluding the four days of debate on the schema as a whole, and later and more explicitly, Archbishop Dearden of Detroit, speaking on behalf of the CM when he introduced article 21 in the *aula*—made it clear that Pope Paul had decided to reserve to himself the issue of birth control and did not wish the council to pronounce on it. Thus any decision on this crucial and very topical issue—resulting from the recent discovery and development of the contraceptive pill—was withdrawn from the council's competence and the road was taken that would eventually lead in 1968 to *Humanae Vitae*, the papal encyclical prohibiting artificial means of birth control.

Archbishop Dearden, in his introductory speech, indicated that the article was intended to be pastoral rather than doctrinal, not "a full treatment of the doctrine of marriage, rather a synthesis of teaching to help Christians today to live their vocation to holiness more efficaciously." Despite the archbishop's statement about the pope's wishes regarding the issue of birth control, the topic remained close to the surface of the debate, indeed almost dominated it alongside the allied issue of the "ends" (Latin, *fines*) of marriage. Regarding the latter, there was general agreement that there were two principal ends: first, the procreation and bringing up of children; second, and put together somewhat incongruously, the mutual help that the spouses give to each other and the remedy for concupiscence—as the manuals of moral theology upon which the bishops would have been brought up in their seminary days expressed the matter. But there was sharp disagreement as to whether the latter end was secondary or, rather, of equal importance with the first. The divisions largely followed A and B lines. The result was a particularly lively, indeed impassioned, debate.

On one side were to be found Cardinal Ottaviani of the Holy Office and Cardinal Ruffini, archbishop of Palermo (Sicily), both of whom were members of the CM but who had openly distanced themselves from the schema as it stood. Ruffini thought it gave too much weight to the consciences of spouses in deciding the number of their children and wanted it rewritten with much clearer reference to the teaching of popes Pius XI and Pius XII. Ottaviani noted that he was the eleventh child in a family of twelve and praised his father for trusting so firmly in divine providence! He hoped the article would be rewritten in a way that expressed a similar trust and openness toward God, in place of the present exaggerated emphasis upon the choice of the spouses in deciding the number of their children, which, he said, contradicted the church's traditional teaching.

The other side was represented by Cardinal Léger, one of the early speakers in the debate who set the tone for many speakers who were unhappy with the current teaching of the church. "Anxieties and doubts about marriage are expressed in many regions and by people of all conditions. The faithful—including the more fervent—are pressed daily with difficulties. They seek solutions that are in harmony with their faith but the answers given up to now do not satisfy their consciences. Pastors, particularly confessors, have become doubtful and uncertain: often they do not know how they can and ought to respond to the faithful. Many theologians increasingly feel the need to investigate afresh and more deeply the fundamental principles of teaching about marriage." Léger urged more emphasis upon the second end or purpose of marriage, a love involving "soul and body" and "the intimate union of the spouses."

Other emphases came from outside the West. Bishop Staverman of Sukarnapura (Indonesia), speaking in the name of nine Indonesian and other bishops, emphasized the historical nature of marriage and the experience of the laity. The church, he said, cannot be content with simply repeating previous doctrine, for if it does the teaching "loses its pastoral effectiveness." He urged the CM to co-opt more lay experts, since they "represent married people better than bishops and priests can" and they know better "both the development of our understanding of marriage, conjugal love, fruitfulness, etc., and the evolution of marriage as an historical reality." Two bishops from Africa wanted more attention to be paid to issues that were especially relevant to their continent. Bishop Nkongolo of Luebo (Congo) focused on the importance of free consent when the couple enter marriage, without undue pressure from their parents or family; and on the evils of polygamy, which "gravely damages the dignity of women" and is, among Christians, "a sacrilegious profanation of the sanctity of marriage sanctioned by Christ." Bishop Yago of Abijdan (Ivory Coast) added to the evils of imposed marriages and polygamy those of the abuses of dowries, evils that together bring "so much damage to the dignity of women in our regions"—issues that were important, he said, because the schema ought to address "the whole world, not just the ancient Christian countries."

Time was pressing and after two mornings of debate the council consented to a premature end. Seventeen individuals had spoken and eleven more were waiting when the vote for the conclusion was taken.

Article 22: Culture

Article 22 dealt with the church's attitude toward culture. There was general agreement that the topic was important and must be covered in the decree; there was also agreement that the church was no longer in control of culture, as it has been in times past, at least in Western Europe. There were differences of approach, however, somewhat though not entirely along A and B lines, as to how Christians should deal with the situation, particularly regarding the degree to which they should accept or confront modern culture. Bishop De Provenchères of Aix (France) summarized the two sides of the coin. The article, he said,

> rightly brings to light the positive character of modern culture, the advances made and the good things that derive from them. On the other hand, it is almost silent about what is lacking and to be deplored, the dangers that may be feared from these advances, new responsibilities that arise from them, and the challenges that must still be confronted. The issue is put in a way that is incomplete and too optimistic, insufficiently relevant to the actual situation and not dynamic enough. What is said, moreover, applies more to the richer nations than to the whole world.

Other speeches expanded on points made by De Provenchères. There were many ideas and considerable diversity in the debate. Two bishops from Asia and Africa, Bishop Lokuang of Tainan (China) and Archbishop Zoa of Yaoundé (Cameroons), spoke about the variety of cultures. Every people and nation has its own culture and the church must respect all of them, they both urged, and Zoa emphasized that cultural values are good because they are "truly human" rather than because of where they come from—be it the West or Africa. The latter needs a Christian culture, he argued, in which the scientific values of the West are acquired without loss of Africa's own religious sense. Both bishops emphasized the importance of intellectual institutions in this work: theological institutes, Catholic universities and publications.

The most radical speech came from Cardinal Lercaro, archbishop of Bologna (Italy). As one of the four moderators who presided over the council debates in the *aula*, and apparently the main alternative candidate at the conclave that elected pope Paul VI, he was a very senior and influential figure, so the sharpness of speech and implied criticisms are striking. He thought article 22 was "almost the knot" of the whole decree and that while it contained many good things, an initial step was missing. "First and foremost the church must ever tend towards greater poverty," especially "evangelical poverty regarding ecclesiastical culture." The church, he argued, can confidently renounce, or at least trust less in, the riches of the past that are no longer consonant with today's spirit, such as scholastic systems of philosophy and theology, academic and educational institutions, methods of research, and so on, for these may obscure rather than illumine the gospel. Evangelical poverty, however, must be distinguished from subhuman poverty. It means "not ignorance and a mean spirit, rather sobriety and a knowledge of one's own finitude, an agility of mind as well as magnanimity and boldness." Looking to the future, he urged a new culture and pedagogy in the church in which bishops would be true theologians and spiritual men and the laity, too, would understand theology.

Article 23: Economic and Social Life

The debate on article 23, regarding economic and social life, was somewhat disappointing. Due to time constraints, only seven of the sixteen bishops wanting to speak were able to do so and one of them spoke off the topic. What was said was mostly unremarkable. A general criticism of the article was that it was too short and abstract. There was a difference of emphasis, somewhat along A and B lines, or between what might be called "from above" and "from below" approaches, between those who wanted the article to put more emphasis on existing Catholic social teaching, especially papal encyclicals of the last hundred years, and those who wanted it to begin rather with the present world. Several speakers combined both approaches. Thus Bishop Benítez Avalos, auxiliary of Asunción (Paraguay), speaking in the name of 105 bishops from Latin America, drew attention to the economic, social, and political inequalities of the region, which contained a third of the world's Catholic population. He saw Latin America as a "field of experimentation" for the social teaching of the church and hoped the region would feature in the document as one of the "signs of the times." Bishop Zoungrana of Ougadougou (Burkina Fasio, then Upper Volta), speaking in the name of seventy bishops from Africa and Brazil, also addressed the issue of so-called developing nations. He wanted the schema to propose a new economic and social order founded on a new international morality, as outlined in Pope John XXIII's encyclical *Mater et Magistra*. Whatever is "superfluous" belongs to the poor out of justice rather than as alms, he said. He urged, too, a move away from aid based on economic, military, and ideological considerations, to "true friendship." He reminded the poorer nations of the need to be careful and not to dissipate their resources, to use help given to them for the common good rather than for that of individuals. The council, he said, cannot be expected to give "technical solutions," but it should open the eyes of Christians to the realities of the world.

Article 24: Solidarity among People

The debate on article 24, "Promoting Solidarity among the Family of Peoples," took place on two separate mornings, November 5 and 9. It was introduced by James Norris of the United States, a "lay auditor" (observer) at the council and president of the International Catholic Migration Commission. He was only the second layperson to address the council (the first was the Englishman Patrick Keegan, who had spoken in the previous month in the debate on the lay apostolate). In fact, the preferred speaker was Barbara Ward, author and journalist of

The Economist weekly, but the office of the council's secretary-general, Archbishop Felici, indicated that it would be "premature" for a woman to address the council. Norris was informed of his invitation a day before the debate and with remarkable energy wrote his speech in Latin (in which he was fluent) during the night: it was duly printed and distributed to the members of the council and others in time for the debate in the morning.

His powerful and perceptive address pointed to the ever-growing divide between rich and poor people and countries, even though, for the first time ever in history, the means existed among the richer and mostly Christian nations of the north to eliminate poverty throughout the world. He urged the council to issue a call for action and to establish a "structure that would propose the institutions, relationships, forms of cooperation and ways of acting to obtain the full participation of all Catholics in the worldwide struggle against poverty and hunger."

Other speakers took up various themes in Norris's address—mostly in general terms—especially the need for global solidarity, the growing and scandalous gulf between rich and poor, and the need for structures to respond to the situation. Bishop Rupp (principality of Monaco) wanted more stress on the need for solidarity among Christians themselves, of different nations and confessions, if there was to be greater solidarity in the world as a whole. Cardinal Rugambwa of Bukoba (Tanzania) wanted clarification of the basic principles of solidarity among all humanity.

> The obligation for all individuals and peoples to respect, love and help each other derives from our common nature and origin and our common history of salvation and redemption. The human race is a single family, which comes from and returns to God, who from one human being made the whole human race to inhabit the face of the earth.

As a result, the cardinal argued, radical economic change is required, so that material goods serve the good of the entire human family rather than the profit and greed of a few. Cardinal Šeper of Zagreb (Yugoslavia) turned to an allied theme: the need for the council to proclaim the fundamental rights of people to migrate from one country to another, especially since "the church is by definition a pilgrim in the world." Cardinal Alfrink of Utrecht (Netherlands) used much of his speech to plead that there be no condemnation of Communism: "Our pastoral duty is to look for good seeds even in the Communist world … and not to close the door to sincere and fruitful dialogue." Few speeches made explicit reference to the details of the article in question. Bishop Rupp was critical, observing that the text managed to obscure clear issues and to use many words to say little.

Article 25: Peace and War

Speakers on the final article 25, "Strengthening Peace," were more specific and showed a good measure of satisfaction with the text as it stood. The topic was live. The Cuban missile crisis had been at the forefront of attention during the first period of the council, as mentioned, and the assassination of President John Kennedy of the United States had occurred during the second period, in November 1963. The Cold War between the West and the Soviet Union, and the possibility of a nuclear confrontation, remained real. On the other hand, Pope John XXIII's encyclical *Pacem in Terris*, of April 1963, had given detailed and widely appreciated teaching about how peace might be strengthened and war avoided, thus providing a good basis for what the council might say.

Opinions were generally favorable toward the article, in some cases enthusiastically so. Of the ten speakers, only Bishop Hannan, auxiliary of Washington (USA), was openly hostile. "The whole article needs to be thoroughly amended," he urged. Several speakers wanted the arguments in the article to be strengthened further, especially in the light of *Pacem in Terris*. Cardinal Feltin of Paris wanted a "definitive condemnation of war, especially modern warfare." But, he said, peace had to be "made," not just spoken about, and, as a gift of God, prayed for. All people of good will should be invited to work together for the abolition of arms, the progress of developing nations, and the strengthening of international organizations, especially the United Nations. Bishop Hengsbach of Essen (Germany), representing seventy bishops, spoke in a similar vein. He urged attention to papal encyclicals and to the importance of dialogue both with Catholics and other like-minded Christians and, more widely, with "experts in political, military and allied matters." Bishop Ntuyahaga of Bujumbura (Burundi) saw fraternal charity as the key: only following Christ's commandment of love will change the face of the earth.

The most contentious issue was nuclear weapons. Most speakers who wanted a stronger condemnation of war had nuclear weapons particularly in mind, sometimes in conjunction with biological and chemical weapons. The strongest speech came from Patriarch Maximus IV Saigh. He urged that the assembled bishops, who came from all over the world, could, through their call for peace, "change the course of history and save humanity." Nuclear weapons, he said, will lead to a cataclysm for the world on a new scale and so the former concept of a just war is no longer applicable; the present schema speaks out against such weapons but an even stronger and clearer "condemnation of all nuclear, chemical and bacteriological warfare" is needed. Two bishops, who came from two of the only three countries in the West that possessed nuclear weapons (the third was France), disagreed: Bishop Hannan (USA), just mentioned, and Archbishop Beck of Liverpool (England). They thought the article had gone too far in its condemnation. Hannan argued that the schema contradicted the common teaching of the church on a just war, and those who defend freedom should be praised, not censured. Beck stated that it was incorrect to condemn the possession of all nuclear weapons as "intrinsically and necessarily evil." He added that it was inappropriate for the council to address a "counsel of perfection"—such as unilateral nuclear disarmament—to people in government who have an obligation to defend their citizens: to them, rather, "affection and respect" should be shown.

Conclusion

The long and emotional debate on Schema XIII was finally brought to a conclusion by speeches from Professor Juan Vasquez and Bishop Guano. The former, a "lay auditor" at the council and president of Fédération Internationale de la Jeunesse Catholique, from Argentina, only the third layperson to address the council, spoke in Spanish regarding the role of the laity in the schema as a whole. Paralleling the case of John Norris, the lay auditors' first choice as speaker was Pilar Bellosillo, a Spaniard and president of the World Union of Catholic

Women's Organizations (WUCWO). But the council authorities—in this case the four moderators (Cardinals Agagianian, Döpfner, Lercaro, and Suenens)—again ruled that a woman was unacceptable. Vasquez emphasized the centrality of the laity in the church—"We are the church, we are the world!"—and described in some detail the "lights and shadows" of the world and the laity's role as a bridge between it and the church. Hundreds of millions of the faithful, thousands of millions of those who hunger for the faith, he said, are crying out for the "Christianization of the world, are longing for its unity in a legitimate diversity." Guano spoke briefly, on behalf of the CM, by way of summary. He thanked those who had spoken and promised that their comments, as well as those submitted in writing, would be carefully considered by the CM when revising the text. On the vexed question of whether the decree was addressed to everyone or to Catholics, he replied subtly that its style was different from that of *Lumen Gentium* and that it must be intelligible to all people, including non-believers. At the same time its purpose was "to stimulate the conscience of Catholics so that they, principally, might consider and fulfill their responsibilities in temporal affairs."

The debate had produced an exceptionally large number of speeches and seems to have engaged the council intimately. The interest is not surprising inasmuch as the large majority of those present in the *aula* as full members of the council were diocesan bishops. They could be expected to be particularly interested in the topic in question: the work and mission of the church in the world. The debate occurred at a time of maturity for the council and when the initiative was moving beyond northwestern Europe—which had provided the motor for much of the first and second periods of the council—to the wider episcopate. The sense is of many individuals, from all parts of the world, speaking with confidence and quite freely about issues that concerned them intimately, indeed passionately.

Most of the debate took place within the framework of Christianity and indeed of the church. The laity were treated more within the framework of ecclesiology and a Christian society than within the world. Dialogue with "the world" was supported more in principle than actually embarked upon. Yet it was the debate's mingling of lived experience with ideas, theory and practice, the divine and the human, that gave it weight and appeal.

The appeal of the debate reached well beyond the confines of the *aula*. The interest of the non-Catholic observers was considerable and generally favorable, though with some pointed criticisms. Lukas Vischer, observer from the World Council of Churches, attended the debates and sent reports back to Geneva. He thought the schema's treatment of "signs of the times" was somewhat facile and could lead the church into being dangerously over-confident and ultimately wrong regarding its ability to interpret God's plans, as had often happened in the past; also that it was underdeveloped from an ecumenical point of view. The Hungarian Lutheran, Vilmos Vajta, and Walter Muelder (USA), of the World Methodist Council, were other ecumenical observers who followed the debates closely and sent back reports to their respective sponsoring bodies. Important too were the talks and conferences on the schema that were given to audiences in Rome by various *periti*, most notably the Dominican Yves Congar.

Press Reactions

The debate attracted worldwide notice through the mass media, especially the press. For France, Henri Fesquet, special correspondent of *Le Monde*, provided lengthy and almost daily coverage. His reporting was mostly enthusiastic. "A great debate" was the unanimous verdict of the fathers at the end of the first day, he said, "a new phase of Vatican II had begun." Yet he criticized the "ecclesiastical" and "ponderous" style of the document, especially as it was addressed to the laity and non-believers. *La Croix*, the Assumptionist newspaper, provided almost daily reports with summaries of the speeches, some editorial comments from Noël Copin and Antoine Wenger, and interviews. "Lively and almost general satisfaction" was reported after the first day of the debate. On the other hand, Copin noted the widespread criticism of the document for its lack of theological content. *La Documentation Catholique* and *Informations Catholiques Internationales* also provided extensive coverage.

For the English-speaking world, especially notable was the Redemptorist priest, Francis Xavier Murphy, who, writing under the pseudonym of Xavier Rynne, continued his influential reporting in *The New Yorker*.[10] He, too, emphasized the importance of the debate and the largely favorable reception given to the schema. He paid much attention to the issues of birth control and nuclear weapons, which were especially topical in the United States. The Rome bureau of the National Catholic Welfare Conference (NCWC) Press Service issued daily reports that were syndicated to many newspapers, as well as circulated to the American bishops. Indeed it was from these reports, with their English summaries of the speeches, that many Anglophone bishops who had difficulty in understanding Latin followed the debate.

In Italy, reporting was extensive. *L'Osservatore Romano* carried a long daily report, mostly confined to summaries of the speeches, and usually the activities of the pope were given greater prominence. *L'Avvenire d'Italia*, the most widely read Catholic daily newspaper in Italy, gave very full coverage. This was due principally to the reporting of its editor, Raniero La Valle, who was a member of the "Bologna circle" centered on Cardinal Lercaro. Most detailed were the reports of the Jesuit priest Giovanni Caprile in the fortnightly *La Civiltà Cattolica*, though they were published only after the end of the debate. The Communist newspaper *Unità* maintained its close interest in the council with almost daily articles on the debate, sympathetic in much of its approach.

Frankfurter Allgemeine Zeitung, like *The New Yorker* a widely read secular publication, gave much attention, publishing a dozen or so relevant articles during the weeks of the debate. Five of them featured birth control and two were devoted to the thoughts of Hans Küng and Bernard Häring. The debate also featured prominently in the weekly issues of *Echo der Zeit*. Paul-Werner Scheele, its Rome correspondent, praised the attempt to address modern concerns in intelligible language and to take seriously life in the world, but he noted the criticisms that the document was too "world friendly" and insufficiently evangelical. The German-speaking press was well served also by the daily reports of the three Catholic press-agencies, KNA (Bonn), KIPA (Fribourg in Switzerland) and Kathpress (Vienna), which worked in close collaboration from their joint editorial office in Via Domenico Silveri in Rome.

Press coverage in the Spanish-speaking world was restricted, partly because the schema seemed to undermine the close church-state ties that still prevailed in Spain under President Franco. Thus, *Razón y Fe: Rivista Hispano-Americana de Cultura*, published monthly by the Spanish Jesuits, provided relatively little coverage of the debate in its regular "Crónica Conciliar" by Jorge Blajot. He described Schema XIII briefly, in November 1964, as "a difficult document, inadequate in its theological basis in the opinion of some people" and he avoided the topic subsequently. Proper treatment had to wait until a short separate article on the debate on peace and war by José Maria de Llanos in January 1965 and a fuller article on the schema as a whole by Miguel Nicolau in the following month.

Reporting in the mass media thus brought the debate, and interest in the decree, to a worldwide audience. To some extent, indeed, the debate was created, not just reported, by journalists. Their contribution is essential to understanding the council, and *Gaudium et Spes* more particularly, as "an event." That is to say, the significance of the decree goes beyond the text itself—even while the text remains, of course, primary—to an appreciation of the wider interest it aroused and to the ways in which it was viewed and interpreted.

FINAL YEAR OF THE COUNCIL, 1964–65

Final Intersession: November 1964 to September 1965

The immediate purpose of the long debate on Schema XIII in October and November 1964 was to help the CM with its revision of the text. Already on November 16, five days before the end of the third period of the council, the CM met to consider the debate that had taken place and to plan for the work of revision during the coming intersession. According to various reports of those who attended the meeting, and others, there was general satisfaction with the reception accorded to the schema, notwithstanding the many criticisms made, and with the encouragement given to the commission to continue the work of revision.

The CM was enlarged with several new members, including the archbishop of Cracow, Karol Wojtyła. The work of revision was divided among a number of sub-commissions; Pierre Haubtmann, a diocesan priest and professor of sociology at l'Institut Catholique in Paris, was chosen as editor-in-chief. The sub-commissions met individually or together in Rome and elsewhere on various occasions during the following months—notably at a six-day meeting of all the sub-commissions at Ariccia near Rome in January 1965, which was attended by over a hundred members of the CM: bishops, theologians, and some laypeople. By May the revised text was finally ready for distribution to the fathers in preparation for the forthcoming fourth and last period of the council.

The revisions were extensive and the overall text was much longer. It remained, however, essentially the same kind of document as before. The full debate in the third period provided the roots of the revision. An important development was the incorporation into the decree of much of the material of five *Adnexa*, which had the following titles:

1. The Human Person in Society
2. Marriage and the Family
3. Proper Promotion of Cultural Progress
4. Economic and Social Life
5. The Community of Peoples and Peace

These "appendices" had enjoyed a shadowy existence during the third period. They had been distributed to the fathers together with the text of Schema XIII but, strictly speaking, because of doubts as to how they had been composed and whether this had been done with sufficient authorization from the council, they were not supposed to be discussed during the debate. Inevitably, however, they crept into some of the discussions, especially those on chapter 4, where there was clear overlap with the material of the *Adnexa*. Now, during the revisions of the intersession, these ambiguities and duplications were removed and smoothed out.

Final Period: September to December 1965

Despite the extensive revisions, Schema XIII still appeared to be set for quite a difficult passage during the last period of the council. Opposition to it remained among many A's, including the influential secretary-general of the council, Archbishop Felici. They were joined by a fair number of bishops and theologians, especially from Germany, who in most respects would be identified as B's. In particular, Karl

Rahner, the most influential of the German theologians, expressed himself on several occasions as very critical of the schema on the grounds that its theology was lightweight and too optimistic. On the other hand, support for the schema, and appreciation of what it was trying to do, was widespread, even while—or, in a sense, precisely because—its ambitious nature in trying to cover so much ground was recognized. Appreciation of this kind was expressed by the episcopal conferences of several countries and regions in their meetings shortly before or early in the fourth period.

The debate in the *aula* occupied a number of mornings in the early weeks of the period, between September 21 and October 8. In the event, support for the schema proved much stronger than opposition to it. Some of the complaints focused on externals: the excessive length of the document, its poor Latin style, its repetitiveness. Of the criticisms about content, many that had been made during the debates of the third session surfaced again. For some the approach was still too European and Western. There were pleas for a better biblical foundation. For some it was too optimistic, insufficiently aware of the reality of sin, and therefore in danger of being non-Christian. At either pole were the succinct assessments of the schema made by bishops De Proença Sigaud of Diamantina (Brazil), an outspoken A, and Hermaniuk of Winnipeg (Canada), a vocal B. The former described it as "*Magna Carta* of modern paganism," while Hermaniuk, immediately following him in the debate, portrayed it rather as the "*Magna Carta* for humanity today"! There were renewed requests for an explicit condemnation of Communism, something that had been studiously avoided in the text and would remain so in the final version. It was argued, against the proposal, that the ideology was already sufficiently condemned implicitly in the document, including in its treatment of atheism, and that only harm and the end of any dialogue could come by mentioning Communism by name.

Regarding atheism, a surprisingly forthright speech came from Pedro Arrupe, the newly elected head of the Jesuit order. He argued that atheism was invading the church and every aspect of culture, especially the mass media—including by implication Catholic journalists—and that the church must devise a plan of action to counter this scourge. It seems that Arrupe was following and expanding on recommendations regarding the struggle against atheism that had been made by Pope Paul VI to the Jesuit order during their recent General Congregation. Many bishops as well as journalists—the speech was widely reported in the mass media—saw the approach as too confrontational. Arrupe also called for almost absolute obedience to the pope, an approach that appeared to many to cut across the earlier debates in the council on collegiality—debates that he had not attended, coming as they did before his election as superior general. Various bishops, including De Proença Sigaud, wanted the schema to be better based on the teaching of recent popes, with more references to their social encyclicals. The issue of nuclear weapons was also revisited, with defense of their legitimacy coming notably from English bishops.

There was some discussion of the status of the schema, still usually referred to as Schema XIII. By this time it was clear that there would be three types of conciliar documents in terms of authority: in descending order, they were constitutions, decrees, and declarations. There were the remaining imperfections of Schema XIII and the fact that much of it was treating of issues regarding which Catholic teaching is contingent and changeable—the economy, culture, warfare, and so on—rather than more fixed and certain, as for example in matters of sexual morality. A few fathers, therefore, wanted the document to be outside the rest of the council's decrees or at the lowest level: to be a "message" *(nuntius)* or "letter" *(litterae, epistula)* or at most a declaration. The large majority, however, recognized that it should be a constitution and some wanted "pastoral" to be added as a qualification. Pope Paul VI, it seems clear, wanted the document to have the status of a constitution.[11] As a result, the final title of *Gaudium et Spes* became "Pastoral Constitution on the Church in the World of Today *(Constitutio Pastoralis de Ecclesia in Mundo Huius Temporis): Gaudium et Spes.*" In this way the decree was accorded the highest level of authority by the council while the adjective "pastoral" wisely allowed room for interpretation. Some, mainly A's, saw the addition as signaling that it was less solemn or doctrinally authoritative than *Lumen Gentium* and *Dei Verbum*, which were styled "dogmatic constitutions," or even *Sacrosanctum Concilium*, which was called simply a "constitution." Others saw the addition as implying a difference of genre rather than any lowering of status. Indeed *Gaudium et Spes* could be seen as the crown of the whole council in view of its length and comprehensiveness—the number of issues it touched upon—and because it corresponded most closely, of all the sixteen decrees eventually approved, to Pope John XXIII's original vision of a pastoral council.

Weariness was an important factor in the debate at this stage. There was recognition that the schema was far from perfect, that this was inevitably the case in view of the contingent nature of the issues treated, and therefore the imperfections should not be lamented too much. There was recognition too that the present period was definitely the council's last and there was no time for major revisions such as had occurred after the third period, but only for relatively minor changes and tidying up. There was pleasure and satisfaction that such a monumental task had been undertaken—almost a new type of document for an ecumenical council, especially the attempt to dialogue with the world—and that the results were worthwhile, indeed commendable, and had caught the imagination of the wider public, both Catholic and non-Catholic, as witnessed especially by coverage in the press, gaining there, too, a generally favorable reception. Weariness as the long years of the council drew to a close, and because of the hectic pace of the fourth and final period, as many decrees had to be reshaped and voted on chapter by chapter, article by article, often even sentence by sentence, meant that most fathers were ready to accept more or less what was on the table.

This readiness was first signaled on September 23, only two days after the debate began, when the fathers voted by the overwhelming majority of 2,111 to 44 to accept the present text as the basis for discussion. The rest of the debate, as summarized above, touched upon, for the most part, the details of the text rather than its overall arrangement. Even so, the CM, divided into many sub-commissions, had to work hard between the end of the debate on October 8 and November 10—when the revised text had to be submitted to the council authorities—to sift through and accommodate the points that had been made in the 160 speeches (which were available to the sub-commissions in the form of transcripts) and many written submissions.

The deadline of November 10 was met and between November 15 and 17 the whole text and its individual chapters, as well as many individual articles and sub-sections, were voted upon. Those voting varied between 2,113 and 2,260. The maximum "no" *(non placet)* in any single vote was 144; a good number, up to a maximum of 523 on one occasion, voted "yes with reservation" *(placet iuxta modum)*. Therefore every part was carried by more than two thirds; yet the "yes with reservation" votes especially revealed continuing and quite widespread unease.

The text was then sent back to the CM and its sub-commissions for revision for a fourth and last time. Even then there were some worries in store. There was a final and again unsuccessful attempt to get an explicit condemnation of Communism into the text. The revisers had to take into account a number of observations of Pope Paul VI regarding the decree's treatment of marriage. Between December 4 and 7, the decree, now recognized with the title that would endure, "Pastoral Constitution on the Church in the World of Today: *Gaudium et Spes*," was resubmitted to the council for a series of votes on the text as a whole and on its individual parts. By now the voting (either "yes" or "no"; "yes with reservation" was no longer permitted) was mainly a formality, yet a sizeable minority remained ready to express disapproval. Thus, on December 6, in the vote on the decree as a whole, the voting was 2,111 in favor, 251 against, and 11 null votes. On December 7, the penultimate day of the council, in the solemn and definitive approval of the constitution, the voting was 2,309 in favor, 75 against, and 7 null votes. Immediately after the voting, Pope Paul confirmed the approval and promulgated *Gaudium et Spes*.

PART II

MAJOR POINTS

The structure, headings, and article numbers, of the final version of *Gaudium et Spes* are as follows:

Preface (nos. 1–3)

Introduction: The Condition of Humanity in Today's World
          (nos. 4–10)

Part 1: The Church and the Vocation of Humanity (nos. 11–45)
    Chapter 1: Dignity of the Human Person
    Chapter 2: The Human Community
    Chapter 3: Human Activity throughout the World
    Chapter 4: The Church's Task in Today's World

Part 2: Some Urgent Problems (nos. 46–90)
    Chapter 1: Promoting the Dignity of Marriage and the Family
    Chapter 2: The Proper Development of Culture
        Section 1: The Conditions of Culture in Today's World
        Section 2: Some Principles for the Proper Development of Culture
        Section 3: Some Urgent Tasks for Christians Affecting Culture
    Chapter 3: Socio-economic Life
        Section 1: Economic Progress
        Section 2: Some Principles Governing Socio-economic Life as a Whole
    Chapter 4: Life in the Political Community

Chapter 5: Promoting Peace and Encouraging the
            Community of Nations
            Section 1: Avoidance of War
            Section 2: Constructing the International
                        Community

Conclusion (nos. 91–93)

There is a clear difference of tone between Part 1, which contains
general principles, and Part 2, which treats of more particular and
concrete issues. Some saw the difference as between a dogmatic or
doctrinal Part 1 and a pastoral Part 2. Most of those who saw the difference in this way were opposed, mainly on account of the alleged
absence of doctrine at least in Part 2, to the document having the
highest status of a "constitution." But the majority in the council who
wanted it to be a constitution prevailed, and the adjective "pastoral"
was added, as mentioned (see above, p. 35): hence the description,
"Pastoral Constitution." Regarding these differences of opinion and
the solution, they were summed up in the footnote that was added at
the beginning of the document as an official explanation:

> The pastoral constitution "On the Church in the World of
> Today" contains two parts which form a unity.
>
> The constitution is termed "pastoral" because, while depen-
> dent on principles of doctrine, its aim is to express the rela-
> tionship between the church and the world and people of
> today. As this pastoral aim is not absent from the first part, so
> the doctrinal aim is not absent from the second.
>
> In the first part the church develops its doctrine about
> humanity, the world in which human beings live, and its own
> relationship to both. In the second it concentrates on several
> aspects of modern living and human society, and specifically
> on questions and problems which seem particularly urgent
> today. As a result, this latter part comprises material subject to
> doctrinal considerations, which contain both permanent and
> transient features.
>
> The constitution should therefore be interpreted accord-
> ing to the general norms of theological interpretation and

with due regard, especially in the second part, for the naturally changing circumstances of the matters treated.

PREFACE

The preface sets the tone for the whole document. Particularly evocative are the opening words:

> The joys and hopes (Latin, *gaudium et spes*) and the sorrows and anxieties of people today, especially of those who are poor and afflicted, are also the joys and hopes, sorrows and anxieties of the disciples of Christ, and there is nothing truly human which does not also affect them.

Thus right from the beginning the decree seeks to enter directly into our human condition, not just in an abstract or universal way, but rather personally and individually, to get into the skins, so to speak, of people everywhere, to empathize with us. Of course the Incarnation means that Christianity has always been concerned with humanity. Yet previously, for the most part, church teaching had been more in the form of instruction, somewhat from above, usually by way of applying the mystery of Christ to our human condition. *Gaudium et Spes* begins rather "from below," with us as human beings, fragile yet called to share in divine life. The paragraph continues: we are "directed by the holy Spirit in our pilgrimage towards the Father's kingdom."

It is then clearly stated that the decree is addressed to all people: "The council now immediately addresses itself not just to the church's own sons and daughters and all who call on the name of Christ but to people everywhere, in its desire to explain to all how it understands the church's presence and activity in today's world." The idea that the church has a message for all people is nothing new, of course, yet the directness of the words in going beyond Catholics and other Christians to all humankind appears unique for an ecumenical council and indeed for the church's magisterium more generally. Of the other decrees of Vatican II, moreover, none is addressed so explicitly to people outside the Catholic Church and the wider Christian community.

Gaudium et Spes should be seen as closely linked to *Lumen Gentium*, the Constitution on the Church, even though the nature of the link is not spelled out. Thus the words of the preface, "after exploring the mystery of the church more deeply," clearly refer to *Lumen Gentium* even though this is not stated explicitly. Should *Gaudium et Spes* be seen as a kind of pastoral application of *Lumen Gentium* for the present time? Yes, but not just that, the introductory footnote, mentioned above, seems to imply. *Gaudium et Spes* is a decree in its own right and of a doctrinal nature, at least in part, and therefore it is better seen as standing alongside *Lumen Gentium* rather than subordinate to it.

INTRODUCTION:
THE CONDITION OF HUMANITY IN TODAY'S WORLD

The long introduction sets the scene in an empirical way. It seeks, as its subtitle indicates, to describe the state of humankind in today's world. Its seven sections have the following headings: Hopes and Anxieties; The Profound Change of Conditions; Changes in the Social Order; Psychological, Moral and Religious Changes; Imbalances in Modern Society; Wider Aspirations of Humanity; Deeper Human Questions.

The introduction begins by stating, "... the church has the duty in every age of examining the signs of the times and interpreting them in the light of the gospel." Notwithstanding the large amount of debate in the council (and afterwards) about "signs of the times," this is the only time that the phrase is used in the final version of *Gaudium et Spes*. The "signs," moreover, are considered in a largely empirical way, as descriptive of the current situation in the world, following the usage in Pope John XXIII's encyclical *Pacem in Terris* of 1963, rather than in the more biblical or theological sense of signs of God's impending judgment upon or intervention in the world.

The novelty of the situation in the world is underlined: "The human race finds itself today in a new stage of its history in which fundamental and rapid changes are gradually extending to the whole globe.... History is accelerating at such a pace that individuals can scarcely keep up with it." The novelty is spelled out in a variety of ways—historical, intellectual, social, economic, psychological—and the consequent effects upon religious and spiritual life are outlined.

The results, both positive and negative, the opportunities and the dangers, are described. The criticism of a one-sided and naive optimism is unfair.

> Never has the human race possessed such an abundance of wealth, resources and economic power, and yet a large part of the world's population is still racked by hunger and need, and very many are illiterate. Never has humanity had so intense a feeling for freedom as today, but new forms of social and psychological slavery are on the increase . . .

> In such circumstances the world of today is showing both its strength and its weakness, the capacity to produce the best and the worst as it faces the road leading to freedom or to slavery, advance or retreat, fellowship or hatred.

Despite the openness to the wider world and to historical developments, the centrality of Christ is emphasized. There is no dissolution into religious relativism.

> It is the church's belief that Christ, who died and was raised for everyone, offers to the human race through his Spirit the light and strength to respond to its highest calling; and that no other name under heaven is given to people for them to be saved. It likewise believes that the key and the focus and culmination of all human history are to be found in its Lord and master.

And so the introduction concludes:

> It is accordingly in the light of Christ . . . that the council proposes to elucidate the mystery of humanity and, in addressing all people, to contribute to discovering a solution to the outstanding questions of our day.

The originality of the introduction, and what follows from it in the rest of the decree, is twofold. First, its description of the world and the condition of humanity in the mid-twentieth century: Vatican II, obviously, was the first ecumenical council to have the opportunity to attempt such a description. Second and more profoundly, there is the recognition of historical development itself and of the church's need to take this into consideration in its teaching.

If one compares *Gaudium et Spes* with the treatment of our human condition in the decrees that perhaps come closest to it of the two previous ecumenical councils, Vatican I's Dogmatic Constitution on the Catholic Faith *(Dei Filius)* and Trent's decree on justification, the difference is marked. Trent's treatment is almost timeless. Vatican I allows some development, as in, for example, chapter 4 of the constitution: "So far is the church from hindering the development of human arts and studies, that in fact she assists and promotes them in many ways: for she is neither ignorant nor contemptuous of the advantages which derive from this source for human life...." Nevertheless faith and reason are put into somewhat separate compartments, so that the relationship between the two is almost timeless, as expressed in the same chapter: "The church takes particular care that they [the principles and methods of human arts and sciences] do not become infected with errors by conflicting with divine teaching or, by going beyond their limits, intrude upon what belongs to faith and engender confusion." There is no suggestion that the church's own doctrines might develop as a result of advances in science or other areas of human activity. *Gaudium et Spes* is new, therefore, both in accepting and welcoming the fact that these advances will influence the teaching of the church and in being prepared to enter in detail into gray areas that are recognized to be contingent and historically conditioned.

PART 1: THE CHURCH AND THE VOCATION OF HUMANITY

The general principles proposed in the first part of the decree focus on humanity. Throughout, the human and the divine are brought together. The basic goodness of the former is emphasized, hence common ground is thought to have been found with all people of good will. Yet what is human is incomplete and impels toward the divine. Reciprocally, God is present in all that is truly human. The vision is reminiscent of the older categories of nature and grace, natural and supernatural. Yet the text is studious in avoiding these traditional

concepts of scholastic theology, careful to avoid any compartmental-
ization of the two levels, as if they constitute a two-storied house. The
intermingling is brought out right at the start.

> Impelled by its belief that it is being led by the Spirit of the
> Lord who fills the whole earth, God's people work to discern
> the true signs of God's presence and purpose in the events,
> needs and desires which it shares with the rest of modern
> humanity. It is faith which shows everything in a new light
> and clarifies God's purpose in the complete calling of the
> human race, thus pointing the mind towards solutions which
> are fully human.

Chapter 1: Human Dignity

This chapter concentrates on the individual and our human makeup.
"Believers and unbelievers are almost at one in considering that everything on earth is to be referred to the human person as its centre and
culmination." But Christians go further in believing that we are created "in the image of God." We are not, however, solitaries, "for by
natural constitution the human person is a social being who cannot
live or develop without relations with others." Sin, moreover, is ever
present and must be taken seriously. It produces division within and
among us: "The human person is divided interiorly and the whole of
human life, whether singly or shared, is shown to be a dramatic struggle
between good and evil, light and darkness."

By our human constitution we are "a unity of body and soul." The
goodness of the body is stated clearly, yet the propensity to sin remains:
"We are bound to consider the body, created by God and to be raised
on the last day, as good and worthy of honour. And yet, being
wounded by sin, we experience the rebelliousness of the body." The
influence of the council of Trent's decree on original sin (*Decrees*, ii,
pp. 665–67) is evident. But the human person is far more than a body.
There is the interior dimension that is experienced when we "enter
into the heart where God, the searcher of hearts, is waiting and where
we decide our own destiny in the sight of God"; there is a "spiritual
immortal soul" within each of us.

The chapter then expands on spirituality and soul with three sections entitled: "On the Dignity of Intellect, on Truth, on Wisdom"; "The Dignity of Moral Conscience"; "The Excellence of Freedom." While the excellence of our intellect and the remarkable advances in modern times "in the empirical sciences, technology and the liberal arts" are praised, nevertheless we also need wisdom, which ultimately comes from the Holy Spirit. The phrasing is well crafted and prophetic.

> The intellectual nature of the human person reaches its final perfection . . . through wisdom which gently draws the human mind to seek and love what is true and good, and which leads it through visible realities to those which are invisible.
>
> The present age more than ever requires such wisdom to humanise its new discoveries. The future of the world is at risk if wiser people are not forthcoming. And it may be noted that several nations which are less rich in economic resources are more endowed with wisdom and can make a unique contribution to others.
>
> By the gift of the Holy Spirit humankind attains in faith to the contemplation and savouring of the mystery of God's designs.

Conscience is described as "a person's most intimate centre and sanctuary, in which he or she is alone with God whose voice echoes within them. In faithfulness to conscience Christians are united with all other people in the search for truth and in finding true solutions to the many moral problems which arise in the lives of individuals and in society." In the past the official church often seemed to have all the answers. So the emphasis, in this passage, of searching for the truth with others is remarkable. Even so, the passage continues, conscience can be mistaken either through ignorance or through negligence. Here traditional post-Tridentine moral theology is clearly discernible, though the language is fresher and less scholastic.

Freedom, too, is exalted and the contemporary age is praised for valuing and pursuing it. Yet it can be abused by those who "cultivate it in wrong ways as a licence to do anything they please, even evil." Its full realization is possible only as a gift of God: "Wounded as it is by sin, human freedom cannot fully realise its orientation towards God without the help of God's grace." The theology is traditional, yet the overall balance is much more positive and favorable toward human freedom than had been the norm. Certainly it is a huge development over Pope Gregory XVI's encyclical *Mirari Vos* of 1832, which stated that "it is an absurd and erroneous proposition, indeed madness, to maintain that freedom of conscience should be maintained for everyone," and indeed over the general tenor of the church's magisterial teaching during the century or so after *Mirari Vos*. One notes, too, the obvious influence upon the text of Vatican II's *Dignitatis Humanae* and the debates that went into it.

A more somber note is struck in the next section, "The Mystery of Death." Yet here too the council attempts to empathize with people rather than just to teach. "The enigma of the human condition is most evident when face to face with death. People are tortured not just by progressive suffering and physical pain but also, or more, by the fear of perpetual extinction." Yet Christ has triumphed over death, gaining the victory for us too: "It was Christ who gained this victory when he freed us from death by his own death and rose again to life."

There follow three long sections on atheism. It is described in various forms, from an intellectual denial of God's existence to more practical rejection of God through lifestyle. The speeches in the *aula* on atheism and Communism, especially in the autumn of 1964, are evident as background. It is noticeable that Communism is never mentioned by name. Noticeable too is the fact that the council admits the responsibility of Christians for the spread of atheism either through inadequate or faulty education or through the insufficiency or sinfulness of their own religious, moral, and social lives. The text, moreover, insists on Christian commitment to this life and to the construction of a better world, thus responding to the criticism that Christianity is interested only in the next life.

The chapter concludes with the section, "Christ, the New Human." The theology of Christ as perfectly human is quite traditional, based on the New Testament and the early church councils, as the references in the official footnotes to the text indicate. It ends, however, with an opening to all people of good will and a statement of belief in the widespread activity of the Holy Spirit, both of which are remarkably new.

Since Christ died for everyone, and since the ultimate calling of each of us comes from God and is therefore a universal one, we are obliged to hold that the Holy Spirit offers everyone the possibility of sharing in this paschal mystery in a manner known to God.

Chapter 2: The Human Community

The second chapter looks beyond the individual to the community, to the relationship between individuals and society. It starts by noting the growth in contact among people as a result of recent technological progress—an early recognition of the effects of globalization. But, it points out, technological progress is not enough. Deeper relationships are needed that produce "a community calling for mutual respect for the full spiritual dignity of each person." Christian revelation has much to contribute to this ideal. The chapter recognizes the teaching given by the church in recent times on these issues: "Recent statements of the church's teaching authority have dealt in some detail with Christian social doctrine." This surely refers especially to the social encyclicals of popes, from Leo XIII's *Rerum Novarum* (1891) onwards. Several of them, notably John XXIII's *Mater et Magistra* and *Pacem in Terris*, are cited in the official footnotes to the text. All of *Gaudium et Spes* was much influenced by these social encyclicals, but recognition in this chapter is more explicit.

The chapter then outlines various aspects of the relationship between individuals and society. Most basic is the commandment of love:

> This is why the first and greatest commandment is love of God and of neighbour. We are taught by Scripture that love for God cannot be separated from love for neighbour... "You shall love your neighbour as yourself."... The immense importance of this is becoming evident as people become increasingly interdependent and the world increasingly one.

Some of our dealings with our neighbor are given to us, others are chosen. They are marred by structural conditions over which we have no control as well as by our own pride and sinfulness. Both the communal and the individual dimension are expanded upon. A distinction is drawn between error, which must always be condemned, and the person in error, who may be relatively free from blame. We must, therefore, respect and love our enemies, "those who think or act differently from us in social, political and even religious matters." There is a fundamental, God-given equality of all men and women inasmuch "as we are all created in the image of God, have the same nature and the same origin, have been redeemed by Christ and enjoy the same divine calling and destiny." Yet, obviously, we are not all "identical in physical capacity and in mental and moral resources." Both the likeness and the differences impose upon us responsibilities toward our neighbour and society.

This chapter, too, concludes with a Christ-centered summary, entitled "The Incarnate Word and Human Solidarity." Christ's solidarity with us provides a model for our solidarity with each other in this life, "until the day of its accomplishment when people, saved by grace, will give perfect glory to God as the family beloved of God and of their brother Christ."

Chapter 3: Human Activity

This relatively short chapter focuses on human activity in the world. The point is made again that recent times have witnessed rapid and extensive technological advances and as a result "the human family is gradually recognising and realising its identity as a single worldwide community." Yet many questions come forth. "What is the meaning and the value of this effort? How are all the resources to be utilised? What is the goal to set for individual and collective enterprises?" In answer, there is surprising modesty and hesitation for an ecumenical council: "The church, as guardian of the deposit of God's word, draws religious and moral principles from it, but it does not always have a ready answer to particular questions."

The rest of the chapter expands on these general principles. Efforts to improve conditions of life, as well as more everyday human activities, are, in principle, in accordance with God's design; indeed, Christians are "strictly obliged" to build a better world and to attend to the well-being of their fellows. Yet this means more than the accumulation of material goods.

> People are more valuable for what they are than for what they have. Likewise, all that people do to bring about greater jus-

tice, more extensive kinship and a more human structure to human relationships, are of more value than technological progress. Such progress can provide the raw material for human betterment but it can never achieve it of its own.

The article entitled "Just Autonomy of Earthly Realities" states the legitimate autonomy of the sciences, provided they are conducted "in a really scientific manner and according to moral norms." The approach resonates with Vatican I's treatment of faith and reason in its constitution *Dei Filius*. The article offers, too, a veiled apology for the church's condemnation of Galileo (*GS*, no. 36, including note 7), another instance of Vatican II's humility.

However, sin and the powers of darkness must be taken very seriously in all human activity, which "needs to be purified and completed by the cross and resurrection of Christ." This chapter, too, concludes with a reflection on how all is summed up in Christ. Human activity is brought to perfection in the paschal mystery, and "the new earth" for which we work finds its fulfillment in "the new heaven." Then "death will have been defeated, the sons and daughters of God will be raised up in Christ, and what was sown in weakness and corruption will put on incorruptibility."

Chapter 4: The Church's Task

This chapter reflects on the role of the church in the world. There is no definition of either church or world. Regarding the former, there is some sliding between the two senses of the teaching authority and clerical body on the one hand and the people of God on the other. "World" evidently has the empirical meaning of the world in which we live rather than the Johannine sense of the powers of darkness. The chapter early on makes several references to *Lumen Gentium* and clearly it is to be seen within the context of this document, as an extension or application of it.

While the council asserts the importance of the Catholic Church's role in the world through its teaching and other forms of assistance, it also recognizes the help given by other churches and Christian communities and by the wider secular world. This recognition is a noticeable development, indeed change, over the prevalent official attitude of the Catholic Church until before the council and another sign of a more humble, self-critical, and pluralist approach.

The chapter outlines the help given by the church both to individuals and to society. It is careful to indicate the limits of this help. "The particular mission which Christ entrusted to his church is not in the political, economic or social order: the goal he set it is in the religious order." But the statement is immediately qualified.

> Yet this mission of a religious nature produces a function, enlightenment and resources which can be of service in constructing and strengthening the human community in accordance with the divine law. And when necessary, according to circumstances of time and place, this mission can, and even should, initiate works to serve everyone, especially the needy, such as the works of mercy and the like.

The church is not tied to any particular culture or type of society. Two extremes, moreover, must be avoided. The first is to think that "because we do not have here a lasting city but seek the city which is to come, we can therefore neglect our earthly duties." The second is for people to become wholly immersed in earthly undertakings, "as if these were totally foreign to their religious life, which they regard as consisting solely of acts of worship and the fulfilling of certain moral obligations." The warning is stark: "The split between the faith which they [Christians] profess and the daily lives of many people is to be counted as among the more serious misconceptions of our day."

The chapter returns to the theme of the relative autonomy of the laity in "secular duties and activities." The laity may expect from the clergy in these areas help but not "a ready answer to every problem that arises." It ends with a christological reflection entitled, "Christ, the alpha and omega."

> While it helps the world and receives much from the world, the church has only one goal, namely the coming of God's kingdom and the accomplishment of salvation for the whole human race. ...The Lord is the goal of human history, the point on which the desires of history and civilisation turn, the centre of the human race, the joy of all hearts and the fulfilment of all desires.

PART 2: SOME URGENT PROBLEMS

This second part of the constitution treats of five "urgent problems," each with a chapter. All of them had been discussed during the extensive debate on Schema XIII in the autumn of 1964, principally in the debates on chapter 4 of the schema, and in the semi-official *Adnexa*. They had been treated at length in various papal encyclicals of the previous hundred years as well as by Christians more widely. Part 2, therefore, represents the culmination of a century of debate and teaching at all levels inside and outside the church. Nevertheless, the stamp of Vatican II is marked.

Chapter 1: Marriage and the Family

Marriage and the family, the subject of the first chapter, had been treated in article 21 in chapter 4 of the 1964 text and in the second of the *Adnexa*. It was also the subject of a separate document, "The sacrament of marriage," which had been debated in the autumn of 1964 as a *Votum* (that is to say, a text that was not intended to become an officially promulgated decree of the council but rather a document that would be submitted to the pope for his consideration and as background for the proposed revision of the Code of Canon Law).[12] Of papal teaching, most important was Pius XI's encyclical *Casti Connubii*, which is frequently cited in the chapter, and various letters and addresses of Pius XII.

Describing its aim as "highlighting some major features of the church's teaching," the chapter reveals a traditional intent and one that is selective rather than comprehensive. The tone and some of the approaches specific to the council are also evident. The biblical foundations, in both the Old and New Testament, for the holiness and central importance of marriage and the family are documented in the text and footnotes. Regarding the two ends of marriage—the procreation and bringing up of children and, second, the mutual help that spouses give to each other and the remedy for concupiscence—which had provoked sharp debate in 1964, both are mentioned in a discreet way and without entering into the thorny issue of the priority of one over the other.

Of their nature marriage and married love are directed towards
the begetting and bringing up of children....Marriage, however, was not instituted just for procreation. The very nature of
an unbreakable covenant between persons and the good of the
offspring also demand that the mutual love of the partners
should be rightly expressed and should develop and mature."

Emphasis is upon the nuclear family: father, mother, and children.
The responsibilities of each are touched upon and "the legitimate
advancement of women in society" is defended. The support given to
married couples and their families by doctors, psychologists, priests,
and others is outlined.

The great omission in the chapter is any mention of the contraceptive (birth control) pill, which was a matter of intimate concern for
many young married Catholics. The issue had been removed from the
council's competence by Pope Paul VI in 1964, as mentioned (see
above, p. 21). There remain a few somewhat veiled references that
seek to follow the traditional teaching of the church while seemingly
leaving open the possibility of a change or development in the future:
"wrongful practices against having children," "virtuous control of procreation," and, most directly:

Ultimately married couples ought to make this decision [regard-
ing the responsibility of parenthood] themselves before God.
In reaching it, however, Christian couples should be aware
that they cannot just do as they please, but ought always to be
ruled by a conscience in conformity with the divine law, and
be attentive to the church's teaching authority which officially
interprets that law in the light of the gospel.

Chapter 2: Culture

Culture, the topic of this chapter, has been central to Christianity
throughout its history. It is integral to the theology of the Incarnation.
Nevertheless, as a word and concept it had not been much used in the
teaching documents of the church. At the start of Vatican II there was
no developed theology of it that was in any way comparable to teach-

ing on, for example, marriage and the family or the social teaching of the church. In this sense *Gaudium et Spes* was breaking new ground. The topic had been discussed under article 22 of chapter 4 when *Gaudium et Spes* was debated in the autumn of 1964 and it was the subject of the third of the *Adnexa*, "Proper Promotion of Cultural Progress." Yet, while there had been wide agreement that the topic was important and the council should speak about it, no clear line of argument had emerged.

Not surprisingly, therefore, the chapter is somewhat tentative. It begins with a broad definition or description of culture.

> The term "culture" in general refers to everything by which we perfect and develop our many spiritual and physical endowments; applying ourselves through knowledge and effort to bring the earth within our power; developing ways of behaving and institutions, we make life in society more human, whether in the family or in the civil sphere as a whole; in the course of time we express, share and preserve in our works great spiritual experiences and aspirations to contribute to the progress of many people, even of the whole human race.

The rest of the chapter is divided into three sections. The first describes the contemporary situation. Its novelty is again emphasized, "so much so that it is legitimate to speak of a new age in human history." This is seen as deriving especially from the development of the natural, human, and social sciences, technology, and the means of communication. As a result, humans increasingly feel in control of culture, to be its "architects and authors." Here there are opportunities as well as obvious dangers.

The second section looks at the relationship between faith and culture, the many links between the gospel and human culture. The principle that God is present in all truly human activity and creativity is emphasized, as is the principle that we are co-workers, "fashioning everything with God, rejoicing in God's inhabited world, and delighting in the inhabitants." The church, moreover, is not tied to any particular culture. Rather, "loyal to its own tradition and conscious of its universal mission, it is able to enter into a communion with different forms of culture, which enriches both the church and the various cul-

tures." The legitimate autonomy of human culture and especially of
the sciences is repeated, with reference back again to Vatican I's decree
on faith and reason.

The tone of the third section, in proposing various urgent tasks,
is optimistic. Contributions from outside the church are implicitly
recognized:

> Since the possibility now exists to free a great many people
> from the wretchedness of ignorance, there is a more appropri-
> ate duty for our age, especially for Christians, to work for
> basic decisions to be taken in the economic and political fields
> and at national and international levels, to recognise and
> implement throughout the world the right of all to human
> and civil culture appropriate to the dignity of the person,
> without discrimination on grounds of race, sex, nationality,
> religion or social condition.

The importance of education, and that all have access to it, is
stressed. Attention is paid to people who may find it difficult to take
advantage of cultural opportunities, particularly "rural people and
manual workers" and women, who "should be able to play their full
part according to their disposition." We must, too, attend to our
responsibilities toward others. In all this the family is central, for
within it "children are lovingly cherished and more easily come to
learn the right order of things, imbibing reliable forms of human culture naturally as they grow up." The approach is holistic and social
and takes into account recent developments in popular culture.

> Leisure time should be duly devoted to relaxation and mental
> and physical recreation in pastimes and study, in travel abroad
> which cultivates one's talents and enriches people through
> mutual acquaintance, and in sporting activities and events
> which are helpful for maintaining a balance in life, even in
> community, and also for establishing relations of kinship
> between people of all classes, nationalities and races.

Literature and the arts are given special treatment. While attention is drawn to the role and contribution of the church, a pluralist

society is more or less accepted as the norm and there is no attempt to describe or impose a fully Catholic culture.

Chapters 3 and 4: Social, Economic, and Political Life

Chapters 3, "Socio-economic Life," and 4, "Life in the Political Community," may be taken together. Social, economic, and political developments had been closely intertwined in the realities of life during the previous two hundred years, notably in western Europe, as well as in the reflection and teaching of the church. Christians had been obliged to confront the results of the Industrial Revolution, the French Revolution in 1789, the Russian Revolution in 1917, the spread of Marxism and Communism, and many other developments. A series of social encyclicals, from Pope Leo XIII's *Rerum Novarum* of 1891 to John XXIII's *Mater et Magistra*, saw the papacy responding to these developments. The two chapters in question make numerous references to these encyclicals. In a sense they are a summary of them yet there is also a different tone. The encyclicals are principally an application of church teaching to particular issues; the two chapters are more empirical, more descriptive of reality "from below." They describe the situation in the world and then offer Catholic contributions. There is no harking after a fully Catholic society and a certain pluralism is accepted, even welcomed. Neither Marxism nor Communism is mentioned by name. There is recognition that many positive developments have occurred outside the Catholic Church. Indeed, there seems implicit acceptance, even praise, for many of the achievements and values of the Anglo-Saxon world. It is tempting to see the two chapters as steering a middle course between Communism and capitalism. Yet the key is more positive: the centrality of people.

Thus chapter 3 begins by stating that "the originator of all socio-economic life, as well as its centre and purpose, is humankind." It notes the benefits of recent economic advances: "our growing mastery over nature, closer and more developed contacts and interdependence among citizens,... better provision for the increased needs of the human family." But it also lists various reasons for disquiet, most of which are the result of people being ruled by economics rather than vice versa. There are the huge imbalances in wealth in the world, the risks of automation putting people out of work, the danger that "workers are in a sense made slaves of their work." Instead, rather:

> The entire process of productive labour must be adapted to the needs of persons and to considerations of their way of life, particularly home life and especially as regards mothers of families, and always taking sex and age into account. Workers should be afforded the opportunity of expressing their own qualities and their personality in their work. And, while applying their time and energy responsibly in their work, all should nevertheless also enjoy sufficient rest and leisure for their family, cultural, social and religious lives.

The earth's goods are destined for all and the rights of the poor are asserted. "A person who is living in extreme need has the right to procure from the riches of others what is necessary for personal sustenance"; to this is added in a footnote the quotation from Thomas Aquinas, *Summa Theologiae*, II.II, 66 art. 7, "In extreme need all goods are common, that is, to be shared." The customary sharing of goods in "economically underdeveloped societies" (this Western and rather patronizing phraseology persists in the document) is singled out for praise. So too are investment, finance, and what might be called responsible capitalism: "Private property or some ownership of external goods affords each person the scope needed for personal and family autonomy, and should be regarded as an extension of human freedom." Yet public ownership of property also has a place. The chapter ends with a short section summing up economic activity in the reign of Christ: "Whoever in obedience to Christ seek first the reign of God, gain from that a stronger and purer love to aid their neighbours and to bring about the work of justice under the inspiration of charity."

Chapter 4 also notes the importance of recent developments, "profound transformations...in the relationships and institutions of peoples," and is appreciative of many of them, including "a clearer awareness of human dignity,...the rights of free assembly and association, freedom of expression, and freedom of religious profession both privately and publicly." This is a long way from the teaching of Pope Gregory XVI in his encyclical *Mirari Vos*, mentioned earlier, or of Pius IX in his *Syllabus of Errors* of 1864, which condemned the proposition that the pope "can and ought to reconcile and adjust himself with progress, liberalism and modern civilization." The chapter in *Gaudium et Spes* continues:

> There is no better way to renew a genuinely human political
> life than to encourage an inner sense of justice and of good
> will and service for the common good, and to strengthen basic
> convictions on the true nature of the political community as
> well as the purpose, the right use and the limitations of public
> authority.

The implications of this statement are then spelled out. A variety of opinions in political matters is to be expected: "People who join in the political community are many and varied and they can legitimately differ in their views." Political and juridical structures rightly vary "according to the differing characters of peoples and historical progress; but they should always aim at forming people of culture, peace and good will towards all, to the advantage of the entire human family." Both obedience to legitimate authority and resistance are weighed. A balance is struck between state intervention and socialization on the one hand and personal autonomy on the other. In a similar vein:

> Citizens individually and together should take care not to
> concede too much power to the public authority nor make
> inappropriate claims on it for excessive benefits and services,
> in such a way as to weaken the responsibilities of individuals,
> families and social groupings.

While patriotism is praised, narrow nationalism meets its just censure:

> Citizens should generously and faithfully practise loyalty to
> their own country, but without narrow-mindedness, and
> should always at the same time look to the good of the entire
> human family which is united by various connections between
> races, peoples and nations.

The chapter ends with a section entitled, "The Political Community and the Church." It appears strongly influenced by the separation of church and state in the United States and seems to eschew the ideal of a Catholic state that was close to the heart of many in Europe and South America.

> By virtue of its commission and competence the church is not identified in any way with political society or bound to any political system, being both a sign and a safeguard of the transcendence of the human person. The political community and the church are independent of each other and autonomous in their respective spheres of activity.

Chapter 5: Peace, Avoiding War, and the International Community

This chapter carries the positive title "Promoting Peace and Encouraging the Community of Nations," yet much of it concerns the avoidance of war. The issues were topical and closely felt during the council. Most of the bishops had lived through the two World Wars of 1914–18 and 1939–45. The Cold War between West and East, principally between the two superpowers, the United States and the Soviet Union, had dominated much of international politics subsequently and the possibility of this developing into outright and nuclear war had come vividly to the fore with the Cuban missile crisis in the middle of the first period of the council. Pope John XXIII had published the encyclical *Pacem in Terris* in April 1963, which had addressed the issues very directly and had been well and widely received. There had also been Pope Paul VI's address to the United Nations Assembly in New York in October 1965. These factors provided a background, almost a foreground, to the chapter. Within the council itself, the issues had been addressed in article 25 of chapter 4 of Schema XVII, in the debates thereon in the autumn of 1964, and in the fifth of the *Adnexa*.

The chapter emphasizes the continuing threat of war, which it describes as a "supreme test as the human family advances to maturity." Peace, however, is not just the absence of war. It must be built on justice and a willingness to share: "Peace emerges as the fruit of love which goes beyond what justice is able to provide." There is, too, praise for pacifists, "those who renounce violence in claiming their rights," though pacifism is not mandatory for Christians. The right to legitimate self-defense on the part of individuals and of countries, through their governments, is protected.

"Total war" is seen as a largely new phenomenon, due to the proliferation of new kinds of weapons. The horrific prospects, especially in terms of the slaughter of innocent civilians, are outlined. "All these considerations force us to submit war to an entirely fresh scrutiny"— an admission that the church's longstanding teaching about a just war needs to take into consideration the new situation. The arms race comes in for strong condemnation. It is "not a safe path to preserving a stable peace." Indeed through the wealth spent on acquiring arms it becomes "a virulent plague for humanity and does intolerable harm to the poor."

The chapter looks forward to a total ban on war: "We must use all our resources to create a time when nations can agree to a complete ban on all war." The foreseen time is in the future rather than the present. The language is perhaps a little weaker than that in *Pacem in Terris*. Still, it is much stronger than that of any previous ecumenical council. The danger is that humankind "may be brought tragically to the point when the only peace it finds will be the dreadful peace of death."

The second section of the chapter treats more positively of constructing the international community. The titles of the articles indicate the contents: "The Community of Nations and International Bodies," "International Cooperation in the Economic Field," "International Cooperation on Population Growth," "The Responsibility of Christians to Offer Aid," "The Active Presence of the Church in the International Community," "The Part Played by Christians in International Institutions." The pluralist situation in the world is accepted. There is no attempt to impose more specifically Catholic social teaching on others. At the same time, Christians (sometimes the text speaks of Christians, sometimes more specifically of Catholics) have an important contribution to make and they are encouraged to take their roles seriously, in cooperation with others. Catholic social teaching, moreover, is seen as based on the natural law and to this extent valid for all. In terms of international bodies, the references are generic rather than specific: it is noticeable that the United Nations is not mentioned by name.

CONCLUSION

The short conclusion brings together various features of *Gaudium et Spes*, especially regarding its general approach. It states again that *Gaudium et Spes* is addressed to all people, not just Catholics and Christians: "All that this council is proposing...is intended to help all people in our day, whether they believe in God or do not recognise him explicitly." It repeats that many of the conditions with which *Gaudium et Spes* is dealing are changeable and historically conditioned, and that therefore much of the teaching should be seen as helps and suggestions rather than fixed norms. It stresses again that Catholics dwell in a pluralist world and they should seek to live and work together with other Christians as well as non-Christians, not to isolate themselves. All these points are new for an ecumenical council, at least in tone and in emphasis. On the other hand, the contribution of Christians, and of Catholics more specifically, is not just one among many others. Because the church offers more, it should be a sign of salvation for all.

> In virtue of its mission to spread the light of the gospel's message over the entire globe, and to bring all people of whatever nation, race or culture together into the one Spirit, the church comes to be a sign of that kinship which makes genuine dialogue possible and vigorous.

PART III

IMPLEMENTATION

This is a difficult chapter to write inasmuch as there are no clear-cut criteria by which the implementation of *Gaudium et Spes* can be judged.

The decree was finally approved by an overwhelming majority of the council and then promulgated by Pope Paul VI. For Catholics, therefore, any outright opposition to *Gaudium et Spes*, as a decree of an ecumenical council, would have been a very serious matter. It would have called into question not just the decree but the whole authority of the council. This is especially so with *Gaudium et Spes* since, being a "constitution," it possesses the highest level of authority given by the council.

Unsurprisingly, therefore, there was no formal rejection of the decree on the part of many Catholics. Archbishop Lefèbvre and his followers were the only significant group to go into schism as a result of the council.[13] While they seem to have had little sympathy for *Gaudium et Spes* and the archbishop refused to endorse the decree with his signature at the time of the council, their formal opposition was reserved more for other decrees, principally those on liturgy (*Sacrosanctum Concilium*), ecumenism (*Unitatis Redintegratio*), and religious liberty (*Dignitatis Humanae*).

Once a decree of an ecumenical council has been approved and promulgated, there is no mechanism for further official endorsement by the Catholic Church. For implementation, therefore, it is necessary to look at more elusive aspects of "reception" of the decree.

There are several factors that are partly special to *Gaudium et Spes*. All the decrees of Vatican II are more in the form of extended essays than of the terse statements and definitions that characterized most decrees of the preceding ecumenical councils. But this is more so with

61

Gaudium et Spes than with any other document of the council. Much of its teaching comes in the form of helps and suggestions rather than fixed norms. The principles contained in it are often softened or nuanced with possible exceptions. This elasticity, at least regarding the details, makes it difficult to verify implementation easily or precisely.

Gaudium et Spes, more than any other decree of the council, addressed the wider world beyond the Catholic Church. With decrees that were addressed primarily to Catholics, such as *Sacrosanctum Concilium* on the liturgy or *Optatam Totius* on priestly formation, it is relatively easy to verify whether their specific recommendations—regarding the vernacular language in the liturgy, for example—were implemented. Most fathers of Vatican II would surely have wanted the implementation of *Gaudium et Spes* to be judged not just by its reception within the Catholic Church but also, indeed even more importantly, by the effect it had upon the wider world. There are then, for *Gaudium et Spes*, several levels of implementation to be considered: within the Catholic Church, within the wider Christian community, and within the wider world.

A final point is that much of *Gaudium et Spes*, perhaps more so than any other decree of the council, linked into a well established tradition of papal teaching, principally the social encyclicals of popes from Leo XIII to John XXIII. This relative harmony contrasts with *Dei Verbum*, *Nostra Aetate*, *Unitatis Redintegratio*, and several other decrees, which had to contend with the rather different tones of recent papal and other official Catholic teaching on the relevant issues. Some A's would have liked *Gaudium et Spes* to have been based even more explicitly upon papal encyclicals, it is true. Nevertheless, the closeness of much of the decree to recent papal encyclicals, combined with its relative openness to modernity, meant a certain marriage of A and B interests and approaches. This was an obvious strength of *Gaudium et Spes* at the time of the council. Regarding the subsequent implementation, it provided an additional reason why very few, at least initially and within the Catholic Church, would openly challenge the document as a whole.

GAUDIUM ET SPES AS A WHOLE

Before examining the implementation of the individual parts of *Gaudium et Spes*, it is right to look at the reception given to the document as a whole. *Gaudium et Spes*, perhaps most of all Vatican II's decrees, was more than the sum of its parts. Its importance, at least as this was subsequently perceived, lay even more in its overall tone and approach than in the details of what it said.

Gaudium et Spes, by any criteria, must be considered one of the council's most important decrees. In terms of formal authority, it was one of the four documents with the highest grade: a "constitution" alongside *Sacrosanctum Concilium*, *Lumen Gentium*, and *Dei Verbum*. It was the longest of the council's sixteen decrees, more than a quarter longer than *Lumen Gentium* and more than twice as long as any other decree. While *Lumen Gentium* and *Dei Verbum* may have contained more theological weight, *Gaudium et Spes* was considered by many at the time to be the crown of the council, the decree that most closely and successfully corresponded to Pope John's intention of a pastoral council.

These factors have carried over into the implementation of the decree. It has continued to be considered a central document of the council. If anything, its authority has grown. The other three "constitutions" may have had the most immediate impact. Still, the inspiration of two of them may have diminished as interpretation has become disputed: different interpretations of *Sacrosanctum Concilium* regarding reform of the liturgy; different interpretations of the relationship between pope and bishops, clergy and laity, in the case of *Lumen Gentium*. As for *Dei Verbum*, its innovations have been taken on board and are now almost taken for granted. *Gaudium et Spes* has retained its freshness, has remained a beacon and point of reference both inside and outside the Catholic Church.

Indeed, *Gaudium et Spes* has perhaps more than any decree come to sum up Vatican II. For biblical studies *Dei Verbum* remains the most important; for ecclesiology *Lumen Gentium*, *Unitatis Redintegratio*, *Nostra Aetate*, and *Dignitatis Humanae* remain fundamental. But in terms of popular imagination, of the church as the people of God, *Gaudium et Spes* probably remains the best known decree. It best sums up the spirit of the council. This is important because Vatican II must be seen as an "event" whose significance goes beyond the contents of its decrees, and in the implementation or reception of this "event" *Gaudium et Spes* has played a unique role through its hold on popular attention.

These are my thoughts as one who lived through the council and has taken an interest in it ever since. One way to a more precise verification is through the literature.

Literature

An essential aspect of the implementation of Vatican II was the publication of the council's decrees. For the English-speaking world, the best known collections have been *The Documents of Vatican II*, edited by Walter Abbott; *Vatican Council II*, edited by Austin Flannery; and the booklets published by Catholic Truth Society (CTS) of London and Dublin. The first two works contain an English translation of all sixteen decrees of the council and both were published in affordable paperback versions. "Abbott" first appeared in 1966, within a year of the end of the council. It immediately became a best-seller and went through many reprints. "Flannery" was first published in 1975 and had already reached its fifth printing in 1980. Since both works contain all the council's decrees, it is impossible to say more precisely how important *Gaudium et Spes* was to those who bought the two paperbacks, though one may reasonably assume that it contributed significantly to the popularity of both works. CTS informed me that the time-spans of the print-runs of the four "constitutions" that were sold as CTS booklets, for which the market was principally the United Kingdom and Ireland, were as follows: *Sacrosanctum Concilium*, 10,000 copies lasting from 1967 to 1983; *Lumen Gentium*, 20,000 copies printed in 1965 and 30,000 in 1966; *Dei Verbum*, 15,000 copies lasting from 1966 to 1978; *Gaudium et Spes*, 50,000 copies lasted 1966–74.[14]

The best-known early commentary on all the conciliar decrees was that edited by Herbert Vorgrimler. It first appeared in 1966–68 as a three-volume supplement to *Lexikon für Theologie und Kirche*, entitled "Das Zweite Vatikanische Konzil." Almost immediately, between 1967 and 1969, it was translated into English in five volumes as *Commentary on the Documents of Vatican II*. The whole of the fifth volume was dedicated to *Gaudium et Spes*, the only decree to merit an entire volume. In the immediate aftermath and implementation of the council, *Gaudium et Spes* was clearly considered to be of central importance.

Its continuing role in the Roman magisterium may be seen in the large number of references made to it in the *Catechism of the Catholic Church*, which was promulgated in the original Latin version by Pope John Paul II in 1992 and first published in English translation two years later. There are some 170 references to the decree in the *Catechism*, far more than to any other decree of Vatican II except *Lumen*

Gentium. Noticeable too is the number of encyclicals issued by Popes Paul VI and John Paul II that built on themes treated in *Gaudium et Spes:* Paul VI's *Populorum Progressio* and John Paul II's *Redemptoris Hominis, Laborem Exercens, Sollicitudo Rei Socialis, Centesimus Annus, Veritatis Splendor,* and *Evangelium Vitae.*

Gaudium et Spes has continued to feature prominently in recent surveys of the council. Two collaborative and international ventures are illustrative. The Gregorian University in Rome published in the late 1980s a wide-ranging assessment of the council, with an international team of authors under the general editorship of Professor René Latourelle, SJ. The work was produced in several languages and the English version appeared in three volumes as *Vatican II: Assessment and Perspectives* (1988–89). Of the sixty-four chapters, eight (36–40 and 58–60) focus principally on *Gaudium et Spes* and its subsequent reception. The decree is also covered extensively in the recent five-volume history of the council under the general editorship of Professor Giuseppe Alberigo, which is being published in various languages, including English.[15] The crucial debates on *Gaudium et Spes* in the autumn of 1964 are covered in a long chapter in volume 4 and other volumes treat further and extensively of the genesis of the decree. The bibliography in "Further Reading" (below, pp. 123–26) provides a short overview of the extensive literature (mainly in English) on the decree.

PREFACE, INTRODUCTION, AND PART 1: OUR HUMAN VOCATION AND THE CHURCH

Humanity is the central focus of *Gaudium et Spes*. As stated in the preface (no. 3), "It is around the human person therefore, one and entire, body and soul, heart and conscience, mind and will, that our whole treatment will revolve." The development or change—some would call it a Copernican revolution—from a predominantly God-centered religion to one that takes the human condition much more seriously, and as much more the ground of our theology, is undoubtedly one of the key features of the teaching of Vatican II. In this development, *Gaudium et Spes* plays a central role. Part 1, together with the preface and introduction, set out the general principles.

Much of this first half of the decree attempts to describe the human condition. Regarding its implementation, therefore, there are two linked questions. First, has the decree's description of the human condition been accepted as correct for the time? Second, has it proved to be prophetic regarding developments over the succeeding forty years?

Theology

In terms of the reception of the theology proposed in the first part of the decree, it is worth noting again that, at least for the overwhelming majority of the Catholic community, and also seemingly within the wider Christian community, we are not talking about the possibility of heresy. That the treatment comes well within the framework of Christian orthodoxy is accepted. Questions lie rather in the details of balance and presentation. What aspects need further emphasis and development, how satisfactory is the arrangement and order of the presentation?[16]

This first part of the decree does not intend to address or settle new theological issues. Its purpose, rather, is to match accepted theological principles with the situation of people in the world. Nevertheless, the attempt to match theology with the concrete realities of human existence is perhaps the most appreciated aspect of the entire decree. It has, too, theological implications: a more "from below" approach to theology, one that takes the contingencies and historical nature of our situation more seriously, and is more grounded in them—what has come to be called in some circles "theological anthropology." Edouard Hamel summed up thus:

> *Gaudium et spes* did not reach its full perfection due to a lack of the time needed for a complete maturation process. Even so, the document does have value as foreshadowing future developments, and is very precious for its underlying intuitions, the various pointers it gives, and above all the seeds of growth that it includes and that have borne fruit since its publication.[17]

Most criticisms must, then, be understood within this generally favorable and respectful context—as suggestions for further improvements, which the constitution itself welcomes. It should be said, too, that most of the detailed criticisms and suggestions came from and largely remained within the more specialized academic and clerical circles. In the popular imagination it was the overall tone of the decree that counted most.

A frequent critique has been that this first part of the decree is insufficiently centered on Christ. Luis Ladaria noted:

> Humanity's definite vocation is its divine vocation: therefore, we must refer to Christ so as to understand not only the Christian but also humanity in general. Yet we cannot help noticing that in the majority of passages [in *Gaudium et Spes*] dealing with human beings as created in the image of God no reference is made to Christ.[18]

Yet this may be more a comment about the order within the four chapters than a straight criticism. That is to say, each chapter ends, rather than begins, with a section on Christ: "Christ the New Human" for the first chapter, "The Incarnate Word and Human Solidarity" for the second, "A New Earth and a New Heaven" for the third, and "Christ, the Alpha and Omega" for the fourth. In this way each chapter begins with a descriptive and somewhat sociological approach and the considerations are finally brought together in Christ—this instead of the world and our human calling being seen right from the start through the prism of Christ.

Whatever the merits of the approach, it was intentional. The majority feeling at the council had been that if the decree was to enter into dialogue with "all people of good will," it had to begin with where people are rather than with the assumptions of Christian theology, which might be unknown or unacceptable to most of them. The chapters cannot be accused of theological relativism: that Christ is just one among many saving or exemplary figures. Even though the consideration of Christ comes mostly at the end of each chapter, his centrality and uniqueness could hardly have been emphasized more firmly.

Much the same may be said in reply to the criticism that the first half of the decree is insufficiently biblical. References to biblical texts, it is true, are relatively sparse. But might not a barrage of such texts have put off the very people with whom the council hoped to dialogue? Scripture, moreover, forms the background to much of the decree's response to the challenges of the time, above all in the final section of each chapter where Christ, the fulfillment of scripture, is seen as our fulfillment too in both this and the next life.

The charge that the approach is too optimistic, insufficiently aware of the reality of sin, has already been discussed and considered to be, for the most part, unjustified (see above, pp. 42–44). It has continued to be levelled since the council. A key factor is to remember again that the decree is addressed to all people. The opening words, "The joys and hopes" *(Gaudium et spes)*, as well as most individual sections, begin in a relatively optimistic and upbeat tone. The reality of sin, to which plenty of attention is given, is seen within this positive context. The approach represents both a conscious theological stance and the more tactical consideration of dialogue with others. The Catholic Church had been widely perceived—including by many of its own members—as too preoccupied with sin, in a negative and somewhat obsessive manner. The majority in the council wanted to redress the balance. Maybe after the council the pendulum swung to the other extreme. An almost naive optimism prevailed in some circles and tension has remained regarding the different approaches. Yet on the whole it has been a healthy tension and the new emphases within the first half of *Gaudium et Spes* have made an essential contribution to this growth of understanding and experience.

Finally, in a rather different vein, the approach to the human person has been criticized as old-fashioned, too individualistic and too much based upon an outdated body-soul dualism. Thus, chapter 1, no. 14, entitled "The Human Constitution," states that the human person is a unity of body and soul, but the starting point is the duality rather than the unity, with inevitably problematic consequences. As Rulla, Imoda, and Ridick noted: "While the doctrine of the unity of body and spirit in the human person is clearly affirmed by the council [in *Gaudium et Spes*], one still notes the lack of a new way of giving adequate expression to this unity so as to go beyond the schematism of body-soul dualism." Maybe, they thought, the desired unity is found best in the concepts of the "heart" and "interiority."[19] Chapter 2, "The Human Community," treats of our dealings with and responsibilities toward one another, yet the starting point is each person as an individual rather than the community as such.

These reflections, and suggestions for improvement and for development in understanding, would surely have been welcomed by most of those responsible for *Gaudium et Spes*. They were well aware of the limitations of the document.

Description of the World

The description of the world, and of the human condition within it, that is given in this first half of *Gaudium et Spes* has proved to be, on the whole, notably perceptive.

The pace of change, outlined especially in the introduction, has indeed accelerated in the forty years since the end of the council. The most obvious development has been the extension of this change to the whole world. In the early and mid-1960s, when *Gaudium et Spes* was being composed, the perceived motor of change was predominantly Europe and North America. Since then, while the influence of the West has remained strong, many more centers and facets of change have developed outside it. *Gaudium et Spes* attempted to speak for the whole world even though it has been criticized for being, at least subconsciously, too Western. The striking thing is that the global nature of accelerating change, which the decree emphasizes, while not quite fitting the situation at the time, has come to pass to a remarkable extent.

The introduction's profile of the dark and negative side, of oppression and gross inequalities, has also remained all too true. The inequalities between countries persist and the gulf within countries, between "haves" and "have nots," has become perhaps even more marked.

The most problematic parts of chapter 1, entitled "Dignity of the Human Person," in terms of its description of the world situation, have proved to be the sections on atheism. Although Communism was not mentioned by name either here or in the rest of the decree, it was in the foreground of consideration. The situation has changed radically since 1989. The fall of the Iron Curtain in that year, the subsequent break-up of the Soviet Union, and the decline of Communist regimes in many other parts of the world have dramatically reduced the challenge from this quarter. As a result, there is inevitably a somewhat dated air to the sections on atheism.

However, the omission of any explicit mention of Communism may have been fortuitous. If it had been mentioned, the teaching of the chapter, and indeed of *Gaudium et Spes* more generally, would have been locked into a limited historical situation that has largely passed away. As a result, *Gaudium et Spes* itself might have lost much of its import. An obvious parallel is the absence from the decrees of the Council of Trent of any mention by name of Luther or Calvin or the other figures of the Reformation, or indeed, for the most part, of the Reformation itself. Trent had the Reformation in mind even more than Vatican II had Communism. But in the end the absence of naming may have given both Trent and *Gaudium et Spes* a more lasting relevance. It is a delicate question as to how generic, or specific, ecumenical councils should be regarding the challenges they are confronting. There are arguments both ways and, indeed, the ecumenical councils themselves, from Nicaea I in 325 to Vatican II, have adopted different approaches.

Of the three articles on atheism (nos. 19–21), it is in the second, entitled "Systematic Atheism," that Communism lies most obviously in the background. The first article, "The Forms and Roots of Atheism," with its description of the subtle ways in which denial of God can imbue our thoughts and lifestyle, and its treatment of our responsibility, remains very relevant reading for today.

The descriptive dimensions of the second and third chapters, "The Human Community" and "Human Activity throughout the World," have also proved enduring. Technological progress and globalization are here to stay, it appears. Indeed the speed of advance on these fronts has increased significantly in recent years. Today, however, there is generally less optimism about the benefits. There is more awareness of the dangers, especially of the ways in which globalization can benefit a few but in subtle ways work to the detriment of many.

The fourth and last chapter, "The Church's Task in Today's World," leads into more theological and ecclesiological considerations. On the descriptive side, its portrayal of the Catholic Church's role in a pluralist situation, where Catholics may act as leaven in society, in cooperation with others, without expecting to live within or impose a wholly Catholic society (sometimes referred to as *societas perfecta*, perfect society), has more and more come to pass. Changes in Spain, Ireland, and Poland, to mention but a few countries, have meant that predominantly Catholic societies are rare indeed and even in them there is little desire to impose, or even propose, Catholicism as the official or state religion.

The more humble approach of limiting the authority of the church's voice in the areas of politics, economics, and social theory has, too, effectively been implemented. Some of the reasons are old. The church has never opted exclusively for a particular political or economic model for society, even if it has sometimes come close to it—as, for example, in its long-time support for the *ancien régime*, the alliance of throne and altar that prevailed in much of Catholic Europe before the French Revolution in 1789. The council's acceptance of, almost preference for, a pluralist situation has meant that Catholics form only one voice among many. This voice, too, has become more fragmented since the council. Catholics, influenced by the pluralist and predominantly secular societies in which most of them live, have themselves come to adopt a more *à la carte* mentality. There are also the tensions between North and South, first and third worlds, which Catholics experience alongside their neighbors. In some areas, it is true, Catholics, and Christians more generally, have become more unanimous and insistent, at least in terms of proclaimed policy, for example regarding peace and justice. But in many other areas this has not been the case. Thus the chapter's recommendation of a more modest approach by the church has come about partly for reasons of principle that the council itself adopted, partly on account of historical developments that were beyond its knowledge.

Implementation

To what extent have the recommendations of this first part of the decree been implemented? This is a hard question to answer because the decree eschews so many of the more easily verifiable aspects of Christian witness. Gone, for the most part, is the emphasis upon the church as a "perfect society," upon the ideal of Catholicism as the official and state church of a country, upon the conversion of whole peoples or countries to Christianity, or what might be regarded as the more outward show, even triumphalism, of Catholicism. In opting for a more individual approach, for the importance of Christians listening to and cooperating with all people of good will, being aware of the signs of the times, the decree is placing success in people's hearts and in their individual actions, in the intimacy of God's kingdom, which is known properly only to God.

Whether this move to a more interior and individual approach has proved wise or truly Christian is an issue that will be discussed again in Part IV, "The State of the Questions." What seems clear is that the council correctly perceived the future direction that the world, and the position of Catholicism and Christianity within it, would take. Some people have felt that the council did well to perceive the trend and to recommend Christian attitudes and lifestyles that were appropriate to the new situation. Others have sensed rather that the council, and the Catholic Church subsequently, should have resisted the trend; that in accommodating itself to the growing pluralism and secularism in the world, the council actually contributed to these undesirable developments.

PART 2: SOME URGENT PROBLEMS

While the first half of the decree discussed the calling of men and women in the world in a general way, the second half focused on five particular aspects of this vocation. One chapter was devoted to each of the following topics:

Marriage and the family
Culture
Socio-economic life
Political life
Peace and the international community

Most of the topics had already been introduced in the first part; now they are treated more individually and specifically. The introductory note (see above, p. 39–40) stated that while the second half of the decree "comprises material subject to doctrinal considerations," its purpose is primarily pastoral, "to express the relationship between the church and the world and people of today." How far has this pastoral aim been implemented? To what extent has the decree provided sound and helpful guidelines for people—both Catholics and others, remembering again the decree's stated aim of addressing all people—in these crucial areas of life?

The same introductory note spoke of "both permanent and transient" features in this more pastoral part of the decree. This part especially, therefore, not only seeks to avoid new doctrinal principles, it also accepts that its "pastoral application" of Catholic teaching to the conditions of the time is open to change. As a pastoral application, it takes the form of recommendations rather than fixed norms; in addition, the transient nature means that while the recommendations may be helpful for some time, they may well have to be changed sooner or later as circumstances change.

Nevertheless, this much more "from below" approach, recognizing the importance of the shifting nature of historical circumstances in moral theology, is itself perhaps the most important aspect of the implementation of the decree. Recognition that the implementation of the decree cannot be easily measured, because circumstances will change, and as a result so too will the guidance required, is itself part of the Copernican revolution that has already been referred to (see above, p. 65). The new emphasis in this approach has been widely but by no means universally accepted. Thus, some of Pope John Paul II's encyclicals, notably *Veritatis Splendor*, as well as the *Catechism of the Catholic Church*, may be seen as attempts to redress somewhat the balance, to assert again the permanent principles of morality.

Marriage and the Family (Chapter 1)

Pope Paul VI's effective prohibition against the council discussing the issue of birth control (see above, p. 21), and his promulgation of the encyclical on the subject three years after the end of the council, *Humanae Vitae* in 1968, proved a watershed in the reception and implementation of this first chapter of Part 2, as indeed of *Gaudium et Spes* and Vatican II more generally. Withdrawal of the topic from the council's agenda meant removing the single issue regarding marriage that was most discussed at the time. This inevitably led to a hole in the decree itself and in its implementation.

Humanae Vitae proved to be very controversial within the Catholic community, with large numbers of clergy and laity dissenting from its conclusions about the intrinsic immorality of so-called artificial means of birth control, principally the recently invented contraceptive pill. Inasmuch as *Gaudium et Spes* steered clear of the matter, it might be argued that the encyclical did not affect the reception of the conciliar decree. But in practice the two issues were linked. There was a sense of incompleteness, even inadequacy, in that *Gaudium et Spes* in its treatment of marriage failed to confront properly the single most pressing issue of the day; there was also the question of whether it might not have been better to allow the council to have discussed and spoken on the matter. The fraught reception of the encyclical, indeed, raised many questions about authority that touched both papacy and council. The issues still await resolution.

In other respects the main lines of presentation in the chapter have been generally well received. The details of the teaching are largely traditional, yet the overall tone and sympathetic nature of the chapter, starting right from the chapter's title, "Promoting the Dignity of Marriage and the Family," are new for an ecumenical council. The chapter must be seen in the context of other decrees of the council—especially *Lumen Gentium* and *Apostolicam Actuositatem*—which emphasize the central role of the laity and by implication that of marriage and the family. Thus the council banished the perception—never officially taught yet pervasive in a shadowy way since the Middle Ages—that marriage is a kind of second best, that married men and women are second-class citizens in comparison with priests and nuns. The positive tone toward marriage has enabled the Catholic Church to stay in touch with its own members as well as to speak meaningfully on the relevant issues to the wider world—including to members of other religions: Muslims, Hindus, Buddhists, Jews, and many others—throughout the subsequent forty years when developments have been rapid and extensive. The ability to command proper attention and speak with some authority has become particularly important in recent years as alternative lifestyles—gay, lesbian, partnerships outside marriage, and others—have been promoted in many quarters almost to the same level as family life and marriage. Perhaps the best way to consider the implementation of this chapter of *Gaudium et Spes* is to think how much weaker and less effective the voice of the Catholic Church, and of Christians more widely, would be without it.

Culture (Chapter 2)

The second chapter on "The Proper Development of Culture" has had perhaps the most long-lasting consequences of all the chapters in Part 2 of *Gaudium et Spes*. It must be seen alongside many texts in other decrees of the council that indicate openness to the modern world as well as within the context of the rest of *Gaudium et Spes*, which is the most noted of all the council's decrees for this receptivity. It must also be seen alongside the openness of the council itself as an event, what has sometimes been called the "cultural event" of the council: the more open procedures that eventually prevailed; the international character and composition of the members of the council and of others attending it; the interest in the council on the part of the mass media and of the world community; and in other ways. Nevertheless, it was in this second chapter that the cultural shift was set forth most explicitly.

The use of the word *culture* (Latin, *cultura*) was itself quite an innovation. Previously the Catholic Church had spoken rather of "civilization," principally in the sense of Catholic Christendom. One may think, for example, of the title of the influential periodical run by the Italian Jesuits, *La Civiltà Cattolica* (The Catholic Civilization). *Culture* had been used mainly, rather, in the restricted sense of literature and the arts. Now the word is taken in a much broader sense, one that was more in tune with its then current use in the social sciences: "everything by which we perfect and develop our many spiritual and cultural endowments; applying ourselves through knowledge and effort to bring the earth within our power...." (no. 53; see above, p. 53).

Acceptance of this broader and more secular definition of culture was symptomatic of the council's recognition of the wider world and many of its values. Gone is the attempt to promote an exclusively Catholic or Christian culture. The role of Catholics is rather to participate in and to act as leaven within the many cultures of the modern world.

In terms of implementation, therefore, the chapter, first of all, helped the church catch up with the situation in the world as it then stood. This in itself was an important achievement and one that is easy to overlook in hindsight. It prevented the official teaching of the

Catholic Church from becoming locked into unrealistic hopes for the restoration of a long-lost past. Once again, a healthy way to consider the implementation of the chapter is to consider how much weaker, or out of touch, the voice of the church might be without it.

Second, the chapter correctly foresaw much of the evolution that has occurred since the end of the council. Appreciation of the diversity of cultures in the world, and of the values within them, has continued to grow during the last forty years. As is to be expected, there were many particular developments that the chapter—as well as *Gaudium et Spes* and Vatican II more generally—did not foresee, at least in any detail. Nevertheless, the chapter helped to put the church in the right ballpark, so to speak. It enabled the church to be taken seriously by the wider world at the time and has since provided a framework within which many unforeseen trends have been accommodated.

Inculturation is an example of such a development. Although the word (Latin, *inculturatio*) had been in some use for many years, including in Catholic circles, it does not appear in the chapter or indeed elsewhere in the council's decrees. Its first appearance in an official text of the church came in the "Message to the People of God" of the 1977 Synod of Bishops.[20] Inculturation gradually became one of the key issues of lifestyle and evangelization for Christians. Even though the word is missing from *Gaudium et Spes*, the chapter as a whole, especially nos. 58 "Multiple Connections between the Good News of Christ and Human Culture" and 59 "The Proper Relationships between Different Forms of Human Culture," provided a framework for subsequent Catholic discussion of inculturation and helped the church to move forward with confidence and initiative on the issue.

Some Catholics have felt that the chapter went too far in accepting the cultural pluralism of the modern world and undermined Catholic culture. Pope Paul VI tried hard throughout his pontificate to emphasize the cultural dimension of Christianity. He spoke thus to the Synod of Bishops in 1974:

> The rift between the gospel and culture is undoubtedly an unhappy circumstance of our times just as it has been in other areas. Accordingly we must devote all our resources and all our efforts to the evangelization of culture or, rather, of the various human cultures.

Pope John Paul II established the Pontifical Council of Culture in 1982 as a new department of the papal Curia. While its main purpose was to enable the church to dialogue better with the cultures of the world, it may also be seen as a continuation of Paul VI's promotion of the cultural dimension of Catholic Christianity. John Paul II has also both lamented very publicly the absence of any mention of Christianity in the new Constitution (inaugurated in October 2004) of the European Union and continually urged Europeans to return to their Christian roots. Both policies seem to imply support for more confident expressions of Catholic and Christian culture (corporate expressions, too, not just those of a private and individual nature). Controversially, in August 2004, Cardinal Ratzinger, prefect of the Congregation of the Doctrine of the Faith and dean of the College of Cardinals, expressed opposition to Turkey's entry into the European Union on the grounds that admission of a predominantly Muslim country would weaken Europe's cultural identity, which is rooted in Christianity. His intervention seems to call clearly for a more public display of Christian identity and Catholic culture. Yet the widespread unease with his remarks, including on the part of the Catholic bishops of Turkey, indicate the strength of feeling for a softer and more accommodating approach.[21]

The chapter in *Gaudium et Spes* on culture has thus provided a blueprint for Catholic thought and activity in the forty years since the end of the council, and has proved a catalyst for further discussion on the issues both within and beyond the Christian community.

Socio-economic Life and the Political Community (Chapters 3 and 4)

Whereas the chapter on culture was quite innovative, the next two chapters, on socio-economic life and the political community, were rooted in a long tradition of church teaching, notably the social encyclicals of popes from Leo XIII (1878–1902) onwards. The two chapters produced a close marriage between conciliar and papal teaching. Papal teaching on these issues after the council developed along similar lines, especially the encyclicals of John Paul II. In terms of implementation, therefore, the crucial question is whether the social, economic, and political developments of the last forty years have rendered the approach of these parts of *Gaudium et Spes* obsolete. Was a vision presented that has proved to be a vanishing Utopia?

Some may argue that the two chapters do not attempt to present a vision, a plan for the future world order. They seek, rather, to describe the situation of the world of the time; and there is widespread agreement that the description is well done, even if the perspective is too Western. They make no claims to predict the future. Their intent and strength lie rather in the approach. That is to say, they urge realism about the actual situation, rather than defaulting too quickly to an ideal world order, and they urge Christians to do the best they can in circumstances that are recognized to be fragmented and imperfect. In bringing together a remarkable number of insights and Christian principles, the chapters provide the components for Christians—and many suggestions for others—to think and act in the world of the 1960s and thereafter.

Probing the issues further cannot be done in any simple or uniform way. The world may be conveniently divided around Rome, to the south, east, west and north.

To the southwest, the most dramatic development after the council was the emergence of "liberation theology" in Latin (South and Central) America. Undoubtedly the movement owed much to *Gaudium et Spes*, and more particularly to the two chapters under consideration, with their emphasis on solidarity with the poor, the importance of taking seriously the construction of a better and more just world, and the concepts of freedom and liberation. The decree put firmly at the heart of Catholic concern, at the highest level of authority, issues that were to become central to the liberation theology movement. Almost all the leading thinkers of the movement were Catholics, had lived through the council, and were familiar with *Gaudium et Spes*. Yet the link seems to have been that of inspiration and catalyst rather than of simple application of the decree to the situation in Latin America.

Thus, liberation theology may be seen as a reinterpretation rather than an application of *Gaudium et Spes*: a reinterpretation in the light of Latin America's own social, economic, political, and religious experience. The statements of the Latin American bishops assembled at Medellín (Colombia) in 1968, which are often considered the basic charter of liberation theology, lend some support to this line of argument. Whereas the European church, which had the greatest influence upon *Gaudium et Spes*, may have felt that Christianity had drifted too far away from the modern world and so sought a reconciliation between church and world, the Latin American church, by contrast, felt that Christendom had become too identified with the modern world and its structural injustices and therefore sought rather to break away from it.[22]

Many, too, especially in Rome, felt that the movement was a deviation from the church's magisterium, a distortion of *Gaudium et Spes*, rather than an application or faithful interpretation of the decree. A succession of statements by Pope John Paul II, and by Cardinal Ratzinger as prefect of the Congregation of the Doctrine of the Faith, have warned of the danger. The Congregation in its "Instruction" of 1984 on liberation theology stated sharply: "This all embracing conception (Marxist analysis) imposes its logic and leads the 'theologies of liberation' to accept a series of positions which are incompatible with the Christian vision of humanity." Two years later the same Congregation issued a milder and more friendly "Instruction" and the pope, in a letter to the Brazilian Episcopal Conference, spoke of liberation theology as admissible and even necessary, if properly understood.[23]

To the south, in Africa, social, economic, and political circumstances have, in many respects, deteriorated rather than improved in recent years. Poverty is grinding for many people; the scandalous gulf between rich and poor widens; the continent has been devastated by civil wars; many countries are ruled by dictators who are almost unanswerable to their people. Christianity plays a major role in Africa, especially south of the Sahara desert. The Catholic Church is prominent in many countries. To what extent can the difficulties of the continent be blamed upon the inherent weaknesses of *Gaudium et Spes* or upon failure to implement its teaching?

There are various factors to be considered in any answer. Vatican II occurred right in the middle of the era when the people of Africa were moving from being colonies of European countries to independent nations. Yet the council, and *Gaudium et Spes* more particularly, had little to say about this epoch-making change in the world order. *Gaudium et Spes* has only a passing reference to "nations on the road to progress and recently become independent" (no. 9). The council seemed unwilling to take sides openly regarding the rights and wrongs of the struggle for independence. However, the emphasis of *Gaudium et Spes* upon human rights, the dignity of the human person, and the importance of the political community may be seen as implicit support for the end of colonialism and the independence of African countries.

Gaudium et Spes shows little awareness of how profound and long-standing the travails of the newly independent countries of Africa would prove to be. The decree tries hard to address the whole world, yet the model for much of what it says is clearly Europe. In retrospect there appears almost a simplistic assumption—some would call it naive optimism—that the remedies for Europe can be exported to other continents, including Africa, and all will be well.

Despite these limitations, the two chapters in question provided many insights relevant to the African continent. They emphasize the interdependence of countries and continents around the globe, the importance of mutual help and cooperation, the recognition of imbalances in the world economy, recognition too that the world's goods belong to all, "that the good things of creation should be available equally to all" (no. 69), the legitimate diversity of social and political structures, and the importance of loyalty to one's country.

The Catholic Church, at least in its official teaching, has remained faithful to these teachings. Many recent developments in Africa have been largely outside the church's control and *Gaudium et Spes* is mentioned only rarely outside church circles. The decree must be seen in the context of other decrees of the council that encouraged subsidiarity and legitimate diversity, as well as in the context of the council as an "event," in which the bishops of Africa, especially in the last two years of the council, played an energetic and significant role for the first time at an ecumenical council since the period of the early church. In these and other ways *Gaudium et Spes* may be considered to have contributed significantly to the many fine and positive developments in the African continent since the end of the council.

To the east, the two most dramatic political and economic developments in recent times have been the fall of the Iron Curtain, beginning in 1989, and the resulting break-up of the Soviet Union and its empire of satellite countries in central and eastern Europe; second, the emergence of Islam as a political force on the world stage. Can these developments be linked to the implementation of the teaching of *Gaudium et Spes* on socio-economic life and the political community?

The more direct link is with the fall of the Iron Curtain and its consequences. Most immediately, the Polish bishops, led by Karol Wojtyła, archbishop of Cracow, played a significant role in the composition of *Gaudium et Spes*, and the collapse of the Soviet empire was first triggered by events in Poland, where Wojtyła—by then Pope John Paul II—and the Polish church undoubtedly played a crucial role.

There was also the wider influence of *Gaudium et Spes* and the council. The decree, and in particular the two chapters under consideration, enabled the Catholic Church to speak coherently and in an attractive way on the social, economic, and political issues that were relevant to the countries of eastern Europe. The text, too, was composed in a way that was not overly confrontational with the Soviet-backed regimes in these countries. Communism was not mentioned by name and the two chapters took on board, quietly, some important considerations dear to Marx and his disciples. *Gaudium et Spes*, moreover, was intimately linked in the popular imagination to Pope John XXIII's work for better relations between East and West. It is the decree that was most closely associated with him, that corresponded most closely to his desires for the council.

It would, nevertheless, be wrong to exaggerate the influence of the decree. The fall of the Iron Curtain took a long time in coming: twenty-four years after the end of the council. Whether the softer approach of the council, and of *Gaudium et Spes* in particular, hastened or delayed the events of 1989 may be debated. The role of Wojtyła in the composition of the decree was limited, albeit significant, and his alternative draft was not accepted by the council (see above, p. 10). To see the decree as a full expression of his outlook, and the events of 1989 as its implementation, would be to oversimplify a complex reality. Obviously, too, many of the causes lay quite outside the Catholic Church. Economic decline and over-extension within the Soviet Union, as well as the attractions of the West, made the fall of the Iron Curtain likely: maybe only the timing and manner were in doubt.

Even so, the dramatic unfolding of events in Eastern Europe and beyond form a fascinating aspect of the implementation of *Gaudium et Spes* and Vatican II. Some seeds of the events were surely sown at the council and the two chapters under consideration form its most explicit statements on the relevant social, economic, and political issues. For life in these countries since 1989, too, the decree may have provided insights and some inspiration, especially for Catholics as they have struggled through the difficult period of transition.

Regarding the possible links with the emergence of Islam as a political force, imagination is required for any assessment. There is no suggestion, even in the decree on non-Christian religions, *Nostra Aetate*, that the council foresaw this major development. Conversely, there is little outward indication—still less admission—on the part of Muslims that they have been influenced by *Gaudium et Spes* or other documents of the council. Nevertheless, the political emergence of Islam appears to have been motivated, to a significant extent, by reaction against the West; and the West, in the eyes of many Muslims, appears closely identified with Christianity. The alleged decadence of the West is seen as intimately linked to the decline of Christianity. Has Vatican II influenced the way Christians perceive Islam and conversely the way Muslims view Christians? Has it, in these and other ways, subtly influenced the recent development of Islam itself?

Answers to these questions obviously extend beyond *Gaudium et Spes* to the other decrees of the council, especially *Nostra Aetate* and *Ad Gentes*. Regarding *Gaudium et Spes*, apart from avoidance of any mention of Islam, there is emphasis in the decree on the importance of Christians living together and cooperating with all people of good will, including therefore Muslims. This new emphasis should be appreciated even if the models in *Gaudium et Spes*, including those in the socio-economic and political realms, are subtly and predominantly Western. Whether the council has increased the "Western" nature of Christianity's image in the eyes of Islam, or rather the openings of the council to the wider world beyond Christianity have been appreciated by Muslims, or whether Muslims see these changes in the Catholic church as further signs of weakness and decadence, and therefore as encouraging the political revival of Islam, are fascinating questions best answered by Muslims themselves. Another aspect of the same topic is provided by the chapter in *Gaudium et Spes* on peace and the international community, which will be discussed shortly.

Finally, to the northwest: Western Europe and North America. Although the two chapters made considerable effort to address the whole world, this "first world," as it has come to be called, provided much of the focus. The majority of bishops at the council came from it, including Europeans who were missionary bishops in other parts of the world. The leaders at the council and in the formulation of *Gaudium et Spes*, both bishops and theologians, came predominantly from Europe north and west of Rome. It was there that, in the years before the council, much of the writing on and experience of the issues that stimulated the two chapters had occurred.

In certain obvious senses Christianity and the Catholic Church have declined in these countries since the council. All of them appear, at least outwardly, in terms of socio-economic life and the political community, more pluralist and secular now than then. The decline of Catholic political parties and trade unions, or at least the dilution of their proclaimed Catholic character, are two examples of the change.

Does the move represent a failure to implement *Gaudium et Spes* or in some sense a sign of success? In backing away from the ideal of a Catholic state and society, the decree much reduces the importance of external and corporate manifestations of Catholic presence in the social, economic, and political arenas. This makes measurement, and an answer to the question, difficult. What is mainly recommended by the council, rather, is a more inner and individual witness on the part of Catholics in public life, working too in cooperation with others.

For some, the shift has seemed a mistake, one that has also contributed to the de-Christianization and secularization of Western Europe. A feature of the religious congregations, secular institutes and "new movements" that have flourished since the end of the council has been emphasis on the importance of work and the participation of their members in business and politics. They have intentionally raised the profile of Catholics in these areas of life. They have, moreover, made explicit appeal to *Gaudium et Spes* in support of their ideals. Opus Dei, the Legionaries of Christ, Comunione e Liberazione, Focolarini, and Neo-catechumenate have led the way. Despite their prominence within the Catholic community, however, they remain relatively small groups and seem unlikely to capture the mainstream of the Catholic Church.

It would be wrong, moreover, to underestimate the continuing vigor of Christianity in its traditional heartlands. It retains numerous committed believers and greatly influences many aspects of life, even though in more subtle and less public ways than previously. The partial shift of emphasis from church membership and attendance to the kingdom of God has positive aspects, too. Here we enter areas of the "anonymous Christian," and "anonymous Catholic," that are known only to God.

Peace and the International Community (Chapter 5)

Of all the chapters of Part 2 of *Gaudium et Spes*, the last has seen the most clear-cut implementation, at least in the official teaching of the Catholic Church. The years of the council form a hinge in the church's teaching on peace and on cooperation with the international community.

Christianity has always proclaimed peace as part of the gospel message: "Peace I leave with you, my peace I give to you" (John 14:27). Yet throughout the Middle Ages the church, at the highest level of councils and popes, promoted the crusade as a holy war to free the Holy Land from Muslim control. In the early modern period the papacy continued to support the crusade—for example, at the battle of Lepanto in 1571—as well as many wars of Catholics against Protestants. In the first half of the twentieth century, popes Benedict XV and Pius XII made important initiatives for peace in the two World Wars; yet the papacy gave support to Catholic armies in various conflicts— the Spanish Civil War is the most obvious example. The commitment of the Catholic Church to peace was at best conditional. In terms of cooperation with the international community, papal interest in the League of Nations, founded in 1919, and its successor the United Nations, was at best lukewarm.

The approach changed dramatically around the time of the council, in part due to the new kind of threat to peace posed by the proliferation of nuclear weapons. John XXIII issued his uncompromising encyclical *Pacem in Terris* in 1963 and two years later Paul VI, in the middle of the final session of the council, went to New York and addressed the General Assembly of the United Nations. Both initiatives were well-received by the international community. The last chapter of *Gaudium et Spes*, entitled "Promoting Peace and Encouraging the Community of Nations," makes a neat marriage of conciliar and papal teaching.

The papacy and much of the Catholic Church have followed this line, both firmer on peace and more cooperative toward the international community, ever since. Pope John Paul II tried hard to avert the war between Britain and Argentina over the Falkland Islands in 1982 and the First Gulf War in 1991. He was explicit in his condemnation of the Second Gulf War in 2003. He has been a strong advocate for international peace throughout his pontificate and expressed the hope that war might be banished forever. His apologies for crusades and the persecution of dissenters, carried out by Christians in the past, underline the church's change of attitude toward violence. Though critics of some of its policies, both Paul VI and John Paul II have been firm supporters of the United Nations and its roles in keeping peace and constructing a better and more just world. John Paul II has been particularly insistent of these roles since the time of the Second Gulf War.

The new approach, cemented by the final chapter of *Gaudium et Spes*, has evidently won majority backing within the Catholic Church. That the chapter was approved by the overwhelming majority of bishops at the council indicates its already widespread support among the Catholic community at the time. Many of the bishops indeed wanted even stronger words. A growing consensus on the issues among all the Christian churches shows the ecumenical implementation of the teaching in *Gaudium et Spes*. The forthright condemnation of the Second Gulf War by Rowan Williams, archbishop of Canterbury, is notable in that it appeared linked to the pope's statements and came from the primate of a country whose government, led by Prime Minister Tony Blair, was a vigorous proponent of the war.

Has the implementation gone far enough? The West is still widely viewed from outside as both Christian and aggressive. This may represent mainly economic and cultural aggression but the military aspect is there, too. The United States and the United Kingdom, the two countries principally involved in recent military interventions in predominantly Muslim countries—Kuwait, Afghanistan, and Iraq—are seen as at least residually Christian countries. To insiders they are known to be Protestant more than Catholic, but the distinction between the two is much less important for outsiders. Many Catholics serve in the armed forces of both countries, especially in those of the United States, the world's single remaining superpower. The American role as "world policeman" is much resented in many quarters. Other countries of "Christian Europe," especially France, have intervened militarily, or maintained a military presence, in various countries overseas. Catholic Poland recently sent a large contingent of troops to Iraq in response to a request from the United States.

In short, Catholics and other Christians, prominently but by no means exclusively in the West, have not gone as far in promoting peace and avoiding war, or indeed in cooperating within the international community, as *Gaudium et Spes* urged. The falling-short, however, should not receive exclusive attention. The decree presented high ideals, yet the members of the council were well aware of sin, aware that reality would likely fall short of the ideal, that general principles always have to be translated and adapted to meet actual situations, that there is some distinction between private and public morality, between what an individual may decide to do and what can be expected of a state. The outrages of the invasion of Kuwait and the destruction of the twin towers in New York provided the gravest provocation. Living in a global community, which *Gaudium et Spes* went far in acknowledging, means that we all have responsibilities beyond our national boundaries. At what point these responsibilities justify or demand a military response is a delicate issue, as has been shown by the sharp divisions within the Christian community regarding most of the recent military interventions. What seems certain is that *Gaudium et Spes* has contributed significantly to Catholics, and other Christians, being more sensitive to the issues at stake, and perhaps also more cautious about military solutions. In an era when the full horrors of nuclear war have been and remain a real possibility, even this greater discretion is no mean step forward.

PART IV

THE STATE OF THE QUESTIONS

How do we stand now with regard to *Gaudium et Spes* and, second, what does the future hold? The previous chapter on the implementation of *Gaudium et Spes* brought the story more or less up to the present day and proposes some answers to the first question. Regarding the second, a prophet is needed.

Of all Vatican II's decrees, *Gaudium et Spes* addresses the situation in the world most directly. Its subtitle, "The Church in the World of Today," states this intention clearly. The decree also makes a sustained attempt both to dialogue with the "world" and to open up further opportunities for such dialogue in the future. Yet, as I write these lines, in the autumn of 2004, the prospects look bleak regarding both the situation in the world and the possibility of dialogue.

The attack on the twin towers in New York on September 11, 2001—the most publicized event of the new millennium so far—has set in train an escalation of violence in many parts of the world that may well move still further out of control in the future. Alongside the violence, bad enough in itself, a whole range of other injurious forces have been set in motion or accelerated. Christian cohabitation and dialogue with Muslims, who form almost one in seven of the world's population, has been the most obvious casualty. The gap in wealth between the West and the rest of the world appears ever more glaring. Time, money, and attention that might be directed to building a better and more equitable world are spent rather on defense of the status quo.

The wave of immigrants seeking entry into Europe, as well as the marked decline in the birthrate in many parts of this continent, furnish obvious parallels with the decline and fall of the Roman Empire in the fourth and fifth centuries CE. The civilization of Europe, which was the heartland of the Catholic Church for many centuries, and

which bears much of the responsibility for *Gaudium et Spes*, is under-
going rapid and marked change and this looks set to continue into the
future.

There are also the divisions within the Christian community. In
this respect, *Gaudium et Spes* is closely linked to *Unitatis Redintegratio*
and various other decrees of Vatican II in terms of implementation
and future influence. Despite much progress in its relations with most
other Christian churches since the council, and almost a revolution in
basic attitudes, the Catholic Church has not seen the reunions with
these churches that many hoped for then and for some time afterwards. Indeed the last twenty years or so have seen, in many ways, a
hardening of attitudes on both sides with regard to the possibility of
such reunion. Relations with the Orthodox and Anglican churches
provide two examples of these difficulties. Among a variety of issues,
papal authority has continued to prove a stumbling block for both
churches, and the ordination of women to the priesthood within the
Anglican communion has raised new obstacles to reunion. As a result
of these differences, Christians have been unable to speak with a united
voice and appear unlikely to do so in the future.

The continuing divisions among Christians, however, have affected
the influence of *Gaudium et Spes* less than might be expected. The
divisions have mainly concerned doctrinal matters, those concerning
authority in the churches, and missionary activity. The chief focus of
Gaudium et Spes was on social teaching, and what might be called theology "from below," and the decree has proved to be, rather, a unify-
ing voice and to have revealed a surprising amount of common ground
among Christians, more particularly regarding most of the areas covered in Part 2 of the decree.

There are, too, the limitations within the Catholic Church. John
Paul II has provided a powerful voice in support of many of the concerns of *Gaudium et Spes*. What the next papacy holds lies in the
future. Although the teaching of *Gaudium et Spes* has been generally
well-received, the voice of the Catholic Church has been weakened
in various ways. The recent scandals involving the sexual abuse of
minors, and the negligence of bishops and other church authorities in
dealing with the cases, have detracted from the credibility of the
church well beyond these issues. Secularization has taken its toll on
the Catholic community, especially in the more traditionally Catholic

countries. While the number of Christians continues to grow in many parts of the world, notably in Africa and Asia, the church remains in many of these regions relatively young and even fragile. Among Catholics, too, there is a much greater variety of opinions, indeed polarization, now than at the time of the council. This diversity looks set to continue and probably to grow during the coming century, though it is, of course, to some extent a sign of health and creativity, not just of weakness and division.

It may well be, indeed, that the Catholic Church in the twenty-first century is heading toward another Babylonian captivity. Diminished and shackled in Europe, its principal home for many centuries, it may live as an exile in much of the rest of the world, harassed and threatened.

The Babylonian captivity of the Jewish people in the sixth century BCE produced some of the finest and most prophetic literature of the Old Testament. From this exile came Deutero-Isaiah with its four Songs of the Suffering Servant.[24] If the comparison is allowed, maybe *Gaudium et Spes* will come to be seen as prophetic and comforting for the church of the coming century. Certainly with its move away from the ideal of a fully Catholic society, toward a more individual approach and one that encourages Catholics to work together with others, the decree provides Christians with a framework that appears relevant to the diverse and often secular situations in which many of them are likely to find themselves for the foreseeable future.

In this respect the overall tone and approach of *Gaudium et Spes* is as important as the details of what it says. The details have been discussed at some length in the last chapter, particularly regarding the five areas covered in Part 2 of the decree: marriage and the family, culture, socio-economic life, the political community, peace and the international community. Despite the richness of the teaching on these topics, we have seen that this could not and was never intended to be comprehensive for the time and still less into the indefinite future. The decree itself recognized that it was treating of issues that change and develop in all sorts of ways and that, correspondingly, an ongoing discernment on the part of Christians is required. New issues, too, or at least new approaches and understandings, have emerged since the council and others will surely surface during the century to come. The roles of women both inside and beyond the church, the many facets of globalization, ecology, the rights of people to migrate from one country to another, are among the issues that are pressing today and in forms that were only partly envisaged by *Gaudium et Spes*.

The greatest strength of the decree, for the twenty-first century, is that it faced squarely the issues of its day and did so in a way that was faithful to the gospel and the Christian tradition. Its prophetic role for the future lies very much in its historicity. It is a treasure that can be returned to and drawn upon partly because of its contents, but even more importantly because it gives Christians confidence and encouragement to attempt the same kind of exploration in their own day. In these ways it can provide a comfort and support for the future.

A second strength is that the decree was debated at length and approved by much the largest and most international council in the history of Christianity. Despite unease about its imperfections and omissions, in the end it was approved by the overwhelming majority at the council, indeed enthusiastically so by the large majority, it seems. Other official documents of the church, including notably papal encyclicals, remain important. But it seems likely that *Gaudium et Spes* will remain the more important charter because of the breadth of support for it at the council itself and during the subsequent reception of the council by the Christian community, and because of the wide range of issues it tackled. *Gaudium et Spes* produced a happy marriage of papal and conciliar teaching.

These points may seem obvious, almost trite. Yet in terms of the church's councils, and of its history more generally, *Gaudium et Spes* is somewhat unique. The decree represents the first time that the church, represented in such numbers from all around the globe, sought to enter in detail into such a wide range of issues affecting people in their everyday lives. For this reason above all, it seems likely to remain a point of reference for many years to come.

SECTION II
DECREE ON MEANS OF SOCIAL COMMUNICATION

Inter Mirifica

PART I

THE DOCUMENT

PREPARATION

Inter Mirifica had an early preparation. Of the seventy or so draft decrees that were prepared for the council, only seven were ready to be sent to the participants before the opening of the council in October 1962. One of them—entitled "Schema of a Constitution on the Means of Social Communications"—was the first draft of *Inter Mirifica*. This text, together with the other six that were ready, were bound together into a single volume and sent to the participants in July.

There are several reasons for this early preparation. The century before the council had seen a massive increase in the extent and influence of the mass media. The inventions of radio, television, and films had an enormous effect upon culture at all levels. A succession of popes had shown a keen interest in these developments and one of the last encyclicals of Pius XII, published in September 1957, was dedicated to the mass media. Known as *Miranda Prorsus*, from the opening words in the Latin text (English, "Wonderful indeed"), it had a more informative official title: "Encyclical letter...on the cinema, radio and television." The document had a major influence upon *Inter Mirifica*.

In view of this interest in the mass media, it was not surprising that the "Secretariat for the Press and the Moderation of Shows" (Latin, *Secretariatus de Scriptis Prelo Edendis et de Spectaculis Moderandis* = SPMS) should find its place among the ten preparatory commissions and several secretariats that were set up by Pope John XXIII in the summer of 1960 in order to compose draft decrees for the forthcoming council. The SPMS had links with the Pontifical Commission for Cinema, Radio and Television (*Pontificia Commissione per la Cinematographia, la Radio e la Televisione*), which formed part of the Roman Curia and whose origins went back to a commission for the cinema established by Pope Pius XII in 1948. Archbishop Martin O'Connor, rector of the North American College in Rome, was president of both the Pontifical Commission and the Secretariat; Andrzej (later Cardinal) Deskur was assistant secretary of the Commission and secretary of the Secretariat.

The SPMS comprised forty-six members and consultors, all of whom were bishops or priests. Within this clerical world, they came from quite a wide range of countries and backgrounds and included a number of specialists in the media world, including Monsignor Timothy Flynn, director of the Information Office in New York, and Fr. Agnellus Andrew, OFM, Catholic assistant at the BBC (British Broadcasting Corporation). Fourteen of them were resident in Rome, but overall the influence of the Curia was less evident than in the ten preparatory commissions.

The Secretariat (SPMS) worked with vigor and largely on its own initiative. The *vota* of bishops and others that were submitted in preparation for the council appear to have provided few helpful suggestions. The final draft, entitled "On the means of social communication" and sent out to the members of the forthcoming council in August 1962, already carried the opening words *Inter Mirifica* (Among the Wonders) by which the decree was to be known. It was quite long, running to over forty pages in print and totaling 114 numbered sections. The headings of the various sections indicate the structure:

Introduction

Part 1: Teaching of the Church
        Chapter 1: The Right and Duty of the Church
        Chapter 2: Defending the Objective Moral Order
        Chapter 3: Duties of Citizens and of Civil Authority

Part 2: Action of the Church, or Apostolate
        Chapter 1: Spreading Truth and Christian Doctrine
        Chapter 2: Aids to Spreading Truth

Part 3: Church Discipline and Order
        Chapter 1: Church Discipline
        Chapter 2: Organs of Church Authority

Part 4: Observations on Some Media of Social Communication
         Chapter 1: Press
         Chapter 2: Cinema
         Chapter 3: Radio and Television
         Chapter 4: Other Media

Final Exhortation

Emphasis was upon the church's teaching. This extended to details: "The right of the church to teach and to regulate regarding the media pertains not only to doctrinal principles but also to particular regulations" (no. 10). The approach was from above, starting with the teaching of pope and Roman curia (no. 56) and extending down through bishops and clergy. The role of the laity was to put into practice the teaching given to them, though their technical competence was appreciated. There was strong support for the Catholic media, for their role in spreading the gospel and the church's message, and for the hierarchy's control over them. There was, too, the implicit hope that the church might come to influence much more of the vast world of mass media that lay outside its control.

The right of people to information was acknowledged, but with qualifications. "There is in human society a right to information about everything according to the circumstances of individuals and groups. ... For not all knowledge is profitable, 'but love builds up' (cf. 1 Corinthians 8,1)" (no. 21). The dangers inherent in the media were spelled out, especially falsification or manipulation of the truth as well as pornography and other unsuitable material. Yet the overall tone was quite positive. There was no general demonization of the media, their importance was recognized, and Catholics were encouraged to become involved in them.

The schema was much indebted to *Miranda Prorsus*. It contains many footnote references to the encyclical as well as to other statements of Pope Pius XII. The layout, the approach and the style of the two documents are quite similar. The closeness of the two titles, *Miranda Prorsus* (Wonderful Indeed)/*Inter Mirifica* (Among the Wonders), underlines the dependence.

Another point of context is to remember that the *Index* of books that Catholics were forbidden to read (*Index Librorum Prohibitorum*:

Index of Prohibited Books), with a very large number of works listed in it, was still in force at the start of the council, though its authority and usefulness were already being questioned. It had been inaugurated by Pope Paul IV in 1557 and had formed, through the centuries, the church's most extensive instrument of censorship over the literature of Catholics. It expressed the kind of supervision over the mass media that still found favor in some quarters and helps to explain the schema's emphasis upon the supervisory role of the church. It was effectively abolished by Pope Paul VI only in 1966.

FIRST PERIOD AND FIRST INTERSESSION, 1962–63

The schema was debated in the *aula* for only two and a half mornings of the council's first period (October 11 to December 8, 1962): those of Friday, November 23, and Saturday, November 24, and half the morning of the following Monday (a full morning meant from 9 AM to 1 PM; there was no resumption in the afternoon). The debate, more-over, was intentionally somewhat low key. After the dramatic opening weeks of the council, when divisions among the fathers began to emerge, especially over the schema "Sources of Revelation," and with other major schemas already in the pipeline for discussion, the debate on *Inter Mirifica* was scheduled partly in order to reduce tension. This, indeed, was acknowledged by the two individuals who presented the schema to the assembled council on November 23: Cardinal Cento and Archbishop Stourm, the latter saying openly that the schema had been introduced as an opportunity for "relaxation" *(relaxationis)* after the previous heavily laden days!

As a result of the reorganizations in the first days of the council when the preparatory commissions and secretariats were transformed into ten "conciliar commissions," the SPMS became absorbed—evidently with some regrets—into what was usually known simply as the Commission for the Lay Apostolate (CLA)—the same commission that was largely responsible for *Gaudium et Spes*. The commission's full and official title continued to remember SPMS: "Commission for the Lay Apostolate, the Press, and the Moderation of Shows" *(Commissio de Fidelium Apostolatu, de Scriptis Prelo Edendis, et de Spectaculis Moderandis)*. The CLA consisted of twenty-eight members of whom seven had belonged to the SPMS, including Archbishop O'Connor who became vice-president of the commission. The CLA would be responsible for presenting the schema—along with various others—to the council and then revising it in light of the debate.

Cardinal Cento, of the Roman Curia, president of the CLA, introduced the schema briefly and Archbishop Stourm (Sens, France), a member of the CLA, followed—instead of and at the request of Archbishop O'Connor, according to Cento—with the second and fuller report. Thereafter fifty-four speeches were made in the two and a half mornings, the large majority of them by Europeans, and forty-three written submissions were handed in. The speeches were mainly favorable to the schema and there was general agreement as to the great importance of the matters being treated, regarding both the scale of the mass media and the huge influence they have upon people's lives. Stourm catalogued the media throughout the world as follows: 8,000 daily newspapers with a circulation of 300 million; 22,000 periodicals with a circulation of 200 million; 2,500 films produced annually with cinema audiences totaling 17 billion; 600 broadcasting stations heard by 400 million; 1,000 television stations with 120 million viewers. To the unprecedented scale of the world's mass media, Bishop Sana (Akra, Iraq), a later speaker in the debate, added another aspect of the novelty of the situation, namely that this was the first ecumenical council to address many of the issues.

Most speeches were short and the debate had a rushed atmosphere. Discussion and decision on this important and hugely influential topic was being squeezed into a very short time. There was little comparable to the substantial speeches and development of themes that occurred in the debates on *Gaudium et Spes*, as outlined above, and on several other decrees. Despite the acknowledged importance of the topic, there was widespread agreement that the schema was too long and repetitive, and therefore needed considerable cutting down.

Many speakers doubted whether such practical and non-theological matters were appropriate for a decree of an ecumenical council, however important they might be in people's lives. Archbishop Beck (Liverpool, England) made the point bluntly, even though he had been a member of the SPMS and therefore bore some responsibility for the schema. Speaking privately, as he said, and not as a former member of the SPMS, he declared: "It is wholly inappropriate to discuss such matters in the general congregation of an ecumenical council." His fellow countryman, Cardinal Godfrey, archbishop of Westminster, made much the same point in more moderate language. Beck argued, too, that the schema was unnecessary because everything in it had already been set forth in various encyclicals of Pius XI, Pius XII, and John XXIII—a point that was suggested more delicately by several other speakers.

There was some confusion about the nature and intent of the schema. Was it intended to set forth the authority and content of Catholic teaching in an ideal world where the church had control over the media, as well as to state the rights of the church to proclaim the gospel message? Was its purpose to give pastoral advice to Catholics working in the very imperfect and compromised world of the mass media as they actually existed, or should it try also to go beyond the Christian community and address all people of good will? Bishop Cantero Cuadrado (Huelva, Spain) and Cardinal Léger (Montreal, Canada) wanted the first two approaches to be distinguished more clearly. Some speakers urged the promotion and expansion of Catholic radio and television stations, including Vatican Radio, so that the church could speak with a clearer and more effective voice. A few speakers wanted, rather, more recognition of the vast world of the mass media that lay outside the church's influence and control. Thus, Cardinal Bea (Roman curia) urged more cooperation with other Christians; Archbishop Soegijapranata (Semarang, Indonesia), speaking of the situation in his country where Catholics constituted a tiny one percent of the population, wanted the schema to recognize more explicitly the rights of non-Catholics in the media. Bishops Höffner (Munster, Germany) and Archbishop Duval (Algiers, Algeria) spoke in a similar vein, urging cooperation with other people in an obviously pluralist world. Bishop Ménager (Meaux, France) thought the schema concentrated too much on the church's rights and wanted it rather to encourage Catholics to get involved in the mass media. Bishop Gonzalez Martin (Astorga, Spain) went further in hoping the decree would be addressed to "all people of good will" and not, as in the present text, only to Catholics.

Some speakers thought the schema was too optimistic. Bishop D'Avach (Camerino, Italy) thought it expressed an "exaggerated and ingenuous optimism" and wanted much more attention to be given to the dangers and evils of cinema and television. Bishops Zarranz y

Pueyo (Plasencia, Spain), De Castro Mayer (Campos, Brazil) and Civardi, a titular bishop who drew upon his personal experience as a consultor to the Italian Commission for Films, spoke in a similar way. Abbot Reetz (Benedictine Congregation of Beuron) thought the situation of the media in some respects—he seems to have had pornography principally in mind—was better in Russia than in the West, which was "infected with liberalism and materialism." He regarded influence of the media as "both excellent and diabolical" and wanted Catholics to be encouraged to protest more about the evils.

On the other hand, Archbishop Perraudin (Kabgayi, Rwanda), speaking, as he said, in the name of the bishops of Africa and Madagascar, thought the schema was too gloomy and focused too much on the dangers of the media. It should, rather, stress the more positive side by encouraging Catholic radio and television stations. Archbishop D'Souza (Nagpur, India) reckoned the schema had missed the opportunity of telling the world how the media could be used to solve such widespread and urgent problems as hunger and misery. It was, he said, fearful in its emphasis upon dangers and should instead concentrate on the good that the media can and ought to bring to people.

The debate overall was rather patchy. Most speakers kept to generalities, perhaps understandably so in view of the limited time and the brevity of most speeches. There was plenty of repetition. Yet there was little enthusiasm to continue the debate further or to go deeper into the issues. It was known that the next two schemas to be debated were those on Christian unity and the church and the mood of the assembly was against any further delay. Hence there was no appreciable opposition when the council authorities, in the middle of the third morning of the debate, proposed that matters be drawn to a conclusion. A single vote was then taken on three propositions considered together: (1) The schema is approved in substance; (2) On the basis of the speeches and written comments, the CLA should compose a shorter text that preserves the basic material of the present schema; (3) Material on practical implementations should be treated in the form of a "pastoral instruction" to be issued by a postconciliar commission. The voting was overwhelming in favor, 2,138 to only 15 against.

Various sub-commissions within the CLA duly worked on revising the schema during the intersession between the end of the first period in December 1962 and the beginning of the second the following

September. The text had to be shortened as well as amended in light of the speeches made and the written submissions. The abbreviation was drastic. The document was reduced to a quarter of its previous length: this included leaving out all the numerous footnotes, mainly references to papal encyclicals. There seems to have been some fear on the part of the CLA that if the schema was not presented in a much shorter and simpler form, it might be rejected altogether during the next period of the council: not because it was faulty but rather—along the lines proposed by Archbishop Beck—because the material was not appropriate for an ecumenical council.

The result was the text of *Inter Mirifica* as we have it apart from a few minor corrections. It contained an introductory section, two short chapters (without descriptive headings), and a conclusion. Although it was finished and sent to members of the CLA in June 1963, it was not distributed to the council fathers until after the beginning of the second period.

SECOND PERIOD, AUTUMN 1963

Inter Mirifica had an unusual ride in the council's second period, which lasted from September 19 to December 4, 1963. By early November, as the divisions and lively debate within the council continued, it became clear that the constitution on the liturgy was the only decree that was likely to be ready for final approval and promulgation before the end of the period. This seemed meager success for a council that was now into its second year. *Inter Mirifica* was therefore chosen by the council authorities partly in order to improve the situation. It had been approved in substance by an overwhelming majority during the first period, the suggested changes had been made during the intersession, and the new text now seemed ready for final approval by the council. This would allow for the promulgation of two decrees instead of only one.

Accordingly, the new text was distributed to the members of the council on November 11. Three days later it was voted on without any further debate. There was only a report from Archbishop Stourm on behalf of the CLA. The voting of the previous November had been respected, he said: the substance of the earlier schema had been kept while the length was much shorter. In addition, various small changes had been made that addressed points made in the speeches and written submissions. Thus, some remarks had been added about the importance of lay cooperation and the protection of youth, there was more encouragement to support the Catholic press, and the theater now received explicit mention. Stourm stressed again the importance of the decree, even while admitting its imperfections. It set forth, he said, for the first time at an ecumenical council, the teaching of the church on issues of importance to contemporary humanity—public morality and public opinion, news, and the formation of conscience—and provided a better understanding of the relevance of the media for pastoral practice and the establishment of God's kingdom. Because of the brevity of the text, he said, the document had been reduced in status from a "constitution" to a "decree."

The voting, which immediately followed Stourm's report, indicated a large majority in favor of the new text but a more significant minority against than had been the case the preceding November. The vote on the introduction and chapter 1, taken together, was 1,832 in favor *(placet)*, 92 against *(non placet)*, and 243 in favor with reservations *(placet iuxta modum)*; and on chapter 2 and the conclusion, 1,893 in favor, 103 against, and 123 in favor with reservations. The vote on the schema as a whole was set for the following week and the day eventually chosen was November 25.

This was not the end of the story. The crux of the problem was that while dissatisfaction with the new text appears to have been quite widespread and significantly more extensive than the voting suggested, nevertheless the voting had been carried out correctly and had produced throughout substantial majorities in favor of the two versions of the schema. The council authorities were understandably reluctant in these circumstances to go back on the voting and to open up anew the whole decree. Moreover, the regulations of the council did not seem to permit such backtracking. Many members of the council shared these hesitations even as they became increasingly aware of both the deficiencies of the document and the importance of the topics it was treating. They did not want the council to get bogged down with the decree when it still had so much else to do.

Before the vote on the schema as a whole took place on November 25, several attempts were made to influence the proceedings.

They centered around two petitions. The first, dated November 16, emanated from a group of American journalists who were reporters at the council. It was signed by three of them, John Cogley of *Commonweal*, Robert Kaiser of *Time*, and Michael Novak, correspondent for *Catholic Reporter* of Kansas City, *Pilot* of Boston, *Harper's*, and *New Republic*, and, as "worthy of consideration," by four well-known council theologians, John Courtney Murray, SJ (American), Jean Daniélou, SJ (French), Bernard Häring, CSSR (German), and Jorge Mejia (Argentinian diocesan priest). It was severely critical of the schema, describing it as a step backward and giving a "hopelessly abstract" picture of relations between the church and modern culture: "It deals with a press that exists only in textbooks and is unrecognizable to us" and endows "the Catholic press with a teaching authority and near-infallibility that is neither proper to journalism nor helpful to the formation of public opinion in the church." By November 25 the petition had collected the signatures of twenty-five council fathers: six archbishops, eighteen bishops, and one superior general. In addition, two influential French journalists had written negative reports about the schema: A. Wenger in *La Croix* for November 13 and H. Fesquet in *Le Monde*.

The second petition was dated November 17 and signed by ninety-seven council fathers including Cardinals Frings (Germany), Gerlier (France), Lefèbvre (France), and Alfrink (Netherlands). It asked the CLA to submit the schema to a full review on the grounds that it fell well short of the standard required of an ecumenical council. If this could not be done, and the document could not be thoroughly rewritten, then no schema at all would be better than the present one, they said. In particular, the signatories argued, the document emphasized too exclusively the rights and authority of the church and disregarded the fact that all communication springs from the search for truth and the desire to express it. Catholic laity in the media, moreover, were not given their proper standing and were placed too much under clerical control.

There was drama at the entrance of St. Peter's on the morning of November 25 when representatives of the two petitions attempted to distribute them to the council fathers entering the basilica. An angry Archbishop Felici, secretary-general of the council, intervened in person to try to prevent the distribution, on the grounds that it violated the regulations in force, and he called upon Swiss Guards to support him. The ensuing votes in the *aula* showed a significant rise in the opposition to the schema. After a preliminary vote on some minor amendments to be inserted into the text, the main vote on the schema as a whole was 1,598 votes in favor and 503 against.

Even after this vote, indeed in part because of the substantial numbers that it showed were unhappy with the schema, there were still attempts in the following days to have it withdrawn or subjected to further review. It is clear that various individuals responsible for the running of the council, including at least some of the four moderators (Cardinals Agagianian, Döpfner, Lercaro, and Suenens), had been unhappy with the schema for a long time. But there was great reluctance to set a precedent by allowing matters that had been voted upon to be reopened. Pope Paul VI, who must have been at least partly aware of the situation, declined to intervene. As a result, the final and formal vote on the decree took place on December 4, the last day of the session. The voting was 1,960 in favor, 164 against, and 27 abstentions. Paul VI then immediately approved and promulgated the decree along with the constitution on the liturgy—the only two documents of the council to be concluded by the end of the second period.

PART II

MAJOR POINTS

With some two and a half thousand words in the Latin original, *Inter Mirifica* is the shortest of the council's sixteen documents apart from *Nostra Aetate*, though several others are only slightly longer. It is essentially the text that resulted from the revisions made during the first intersession and was voted upon, without any further debate, on November 14, 1963. It contains a short introduction (nos. 1–2), two chapters (nos. 3–12 and 13–22), and conclusions (nos. 23–24).

Introduction

The short introduction notes that "the wonderful inventions of modern technology" have opened up "fresh ways of communicating news, ideas and directives of all sorts with great ease." The press, cinema, radio, and television are given explicit mention. On the one hand, these media can be of great benefit, if rightly used, "for they can provide much that contributes to relaxation and improvement of mind and to the spread and strengthening of the kingdom of God." On the other hand, their misuse can damage both individuals and society. The purpose of the decree, therefore, is "to deal with the main problems connected with the mass media" and the council is "confident that the teaching and directives set forth in this way will be of service not only to Christians but also to the whole of human society."

Chapter 1

The first chapter, which has no heading to indicate the contents, begins by stating the rights and authority of the church over the media. "The church has a natural right to use and to possess any of the media in so far as they are necessary or useful for Christian education and the work of the salvation of souls." The laity "have a special role in animating the media with a human and Christian spirit," but authority lies in the hands of "pastors of souls" to lay down the principles of morality that should guide people in the use of the media.

The substance of the passage in the first draft of *Inter Mirifica* regarding the right of people to information and the limitations upon this right (see above, p. 95), was kept. It reads in full:

> There is in human society a right to information about matters that concern people individually or collectively, according to the circumstances of each person. However, the proper use of this right demands that the information be objectively true, and complete within the limits of justice and charity. As regards the manner of presentation, it should be decent and appropriate, that is it must respect the moral law and the legitimate rights and dignity of people, both in the search for news and in its publication. For not all knowledge is profitable, "but love builds up" (1 Corinthians 8, 1). (No. 5)

The chapter then examines the "inter-relation of art and morality." Priority is given to the latter: "The council asserts that the absolute primacy of an objective moral law must be acknowledged by all." Individuals must show this by their own free choice in what they read, see, and listen to, and they should keep themselves "informed in good time of opinions voiced by competent authorities in these matters." All, especially the young, should "strive to exercise moderation and self-control in their use of the mass media," and the duty of parents to protect their children from encountering unsuitable material is stressed.

Attention is given to those directly involved in the media: "journalists, writers, actors, designers, producers, middlemen, distributors, operators, sellers, critics, and others." To them belongs "the main moral responsibility concerning the proper use of the media." They are especially reminded of their obligation to young people, "to provide wholesome entertainment for them and to raise their minds to higher things." They are encouraged "to draw up guidelines in economic, political and artistic matters" and to form trade unions that "impose upon their members—by a formal contract if necessary—a proper respect for the moral law in their own sphere of business."

Finally, the decree addresses civil authority. "It must carefully safeguard the true and just freedom of communication which modern society needs for its progress, especially in what concerns the press. It should foster religion, culture and the fine arts...." But it is also "bound to ensure, by the promulgation of laws and their exact enforcement, and by a just vigilance, that the misuse of the media does not inflict serious harm on public morality and the welfare of society.

The chapter is not breaking new ground. It was never intended to. It is a condensation of the preparatory schema, which in turn depended much upon papal teaching of the previous half century or so. But was it abreast of the time or a step backwards? At least to this writer, the document seems more relevant than some of its critics have argued. It maintains the directive role of the church and the importance of the moral law but it does not try to spell out too closely what these involve. There is room for interpretation. Moreover, when the church is understood primarily as the people of God, as *Lumen Gentium* was soon to proclaim, the whole approach of the decree becomes less "from above" and more "from below." The sections on the laity, on all who work in and use the media, make up the body of the chapter and contain much wisdom. Individual responsibility, too, is emphasized.

The chapter appears to be speaking about, or harking after, a world where Catholics—through the authority of both church and state—are directly in control of the media and possess their own press and radio and television stations. But even here the language is somewhat ambiguous. The chapter speaks of civil authority, of Catholics spreading church teaching through the media, and forming trades unions, but it does not insist on pressing the issues in a narrowly sectarian direction. It fails, nevertheless, to recognize adequately the pluralism that existed in the media world, to acknowledge how much of the media lay right outside the church's control or influence.

Chapter 2

The second chapter, which is also without a descriptive heading, focuses more precisely on Catholic media and their role in building up the church and spreading the gospel message. It begins thus: "All members of the church should be of one mind and heart in their efforts to utilize the media, effectively and without delay, in the manifold works of the apostolate, as times and circumstances demand." The chapter then addresses each of the media in turn.

> First of all, a respectable press should be encouraged. A press worthy of the name "Catholic" should be established and developed to imbue its readers with a Christian spirit. Whether it is set up directly by ecclesiastical authority or with the backing of Catholic lay people, it should have the explicit intention of moulding, strengthening and promoting public opinion in harmony with the natural law and the teaching of the Catholic church.

Films, "which contribute to wholesome relaxation, culture and art, especially if they are intended for the young, should be vigorously promoted and guaranteed by effective means." Likewise, "effective support should be given to wholesome radio and television broadcasts, especially those suitable for the family. Catholic broadcasts should be intelligently fostered in order to draw hearers and viewers to a share in the life of the church and to instil religious truth in them." Finally, "the ancient and noble art of the theatre...should aim at educating the finer feelings and moral sense of the audiences." Attention is then given to formation:

> Timely training should be given to priests, religious and lay people so that they may be qualified by the appropriate skill to utilize the media for apostolic work....Lay people need to be trained in art, doctrine and morality. More schools, faculties and colleges have to be set up, where journalists and writers for the cinema, radio and television, and others concerned, can acquire an integrated formation, imbued with a Christian

spirit, particularly in matters relating to the church's social doctrine. Actors too must be given training and support if their art is to be a fitting benefit to society.

Catholics were reminded of their "obligation" to support the Catholic media. Each diocese was to dedicate a day each year for this purpose, when prayers were to be said and financial contributions made. Pastoral care for the mass media belonged first of all to the pope and then to bishops in their dioceses. The decree ordered that "national centers for the press, cinema, radio and television be set up everywhere and encouraged in every way." These centers were to be under the supervision of "a special commission of bishops or a bishop delegated for the purpose," and "lay people, who are well instructed in catholic teaching and skilled in their own profession, should play their part in them."

There is evident in this second chapter, much more so than in the first, the twofold danger of an exaggerated emphasis upon clerical control and of over-reliance upon an ideal world of Catholic media which scarcely existed at the time and was unlikely to materialize in the future. Nevertheless, the encouragement given to the mass media, the recognition of their enormous influence, and the concern for vigorous, creative, and healthy results, should be appreciated.

Conclusions

The brief "Conclusions" recognized the incompleteness of the decree and directed that, in order to make effective its "principles and guidelines," a "pastoral instruction" be later published by a curial office—evidently the Pontifical Commission for Cinema, Radio and Television (see above, p. 93), which had been incorporated into the Secretariat of State, was intended—with the assistance of "experts" from different countries.

"For the rest, this synod has every confidence that its presentation of undertakings and norms will be willingly received and faithfully observed by all members of the church." The decree then appealed more widely to "all people of good will, especially those working with the mass media, to use them solely for the good of human society, whose destiny is daily becoming more and more dependent on their right use." The final purpose was then stated thus:

> So it will come about that the name of the Lord is glorified by these inventions of our own days as it was by the masterpieces of former times, according to the sayings of St Paul, "Jesus Christ is the same yesterday, today and forever" (Hebrews 13, 8).

PART III
IMPLEMENTATION

THE COUNCIL AND ITS IMMEDIATE AFTERMATH

Reception of *Inter Mirifica* began during the council itself. Dissatisfaction with the schema during the second period, immediately before the final approval and promulgation of the decree, sometimes expressed in strong language both by members of the council and by journalists, has been mentioned. Unease with the decree remained during the final two years of the council, even though it was too late to do anything effective about it.

Some sense of the discontent comes from the "Introduction" and "Response" to the decree in Abbott's English edition of the council's decrees, which was first published in 1966 within months of the end of the council (see above, p. 64). The two short pieces on the decree are indicative of its early reception. More than this, inasmuch as the book became hugely popular, running into many reprints and dominating the Anglophone market for a decade as the most reasonably priced and accessible paperback version of the decrees, the work influenced the subsequent reception and implementation of *Inter Mirifica*.

In the "Introduction," the American Jesuit priest Thomas Burke struck a note mainly of disappointment:

> One can speculate that if this decree had been discussed later in the council, after the many sessions devoted to the church in the modern world and to religious freedom, the texture of the decree might have been somewhat richer. As it now stands, it seems somewhat ironic that the church, which is basically concerned with communicating the truth and life to the world, and has shown, especially in the period of the

council, an awareness of the importance of mass means of communication, issued the slightest document of the council on the media of social communication.

He claimed, however, that the decree marked the first time that an ecumenical council had addressed the problem of communication and thought the decree was "more important for this than for its contents." He ended by quoting with evident approval the comments of Gustave Weigel, SJ, at the U.S. bishops' press panel session on November 14, 1963: "The decree does not strike me as being very remarkable. It is not going to produce great changes. It does not contain novel positions, but gathers and officially states a number of points previously stated and taught on a less official level."

More forthright criticism came in the "Response" by Stanley Stuber, director of Association Press, New York, a guest-observer at Vatican II and for many years chairman of the Commission on Religious Freedom of the Baptist World Alliance. He argued that the decree fell "far short of the high standards" of almost all the other documents of the council and was "not only pre-*aggiornamento* (of John XXIII) but definitely pre-Pius XII." Like Burke, he wondered how much better a decree might have emerged if it had been allowed to mature instead of being rushed through in the second period. In short, he said:

> Unlike other documents of the council, especially the Declaration on Religious Freedom and the Constitution on the Church in the Modern World, this decree looks backward rather than forward, inward rather than outward. It deals primarily with one church rather than with Christianity at large. It relies upon outdated Catholic misconceptions rather than upon creative achievements of the secular mass communication profession and practice.

He saw a ray of hope in that the decree encouraged new organizations to be formed within the church to promote the cause of social communication. If the decree was seen as a starting point rather than an end in itself, it might be a blessing in disguise. He took some comfort, too, in the fact that the decree was surrounded by the "progressive spirit" of most of the rest of the council. But on the decree itself his judgment was overwhelmingly negative: "Our modern problem is not the firm control of mass media, but the creative and constructive development of its content"—the decree, he thought, had got it badly wrong on both counts.

How widespread was the negative assessment? The journalists that have been cited above and in the previous chapter came mostly from the United States, where freedom of the press was exalted and the mass media were predominantly secular in character. But criticism was not confined to the English-speaking world. Antoine Wenger and Henri Fesquet, distinguished French journalists, have been mentioned. The press in Germany was also generally negative toward the decree, and the criticism included various articles written by the Redemptorist priest Bernard Häring. Inasmuch as the press corps attending Vatican II felt they were given little cooperation by the council authorities in the early stages, there may have been a touch of revenge in the press's hostile attitude toward a decree that entered so directly into their home territory. But this doesn't explain everything, since relations between press and council improved markedly from the second period onwards and yet dissatisfaction with the decree continued. The twenty-five fathers who signed the petition of November 16 and the ninety-seven who signed that of November 17, 1963 (see above, p. 102) came from a wide range of countries and reveal the international character of the discontent. The fact that none of the twenty-five came from the United States belies the argument that opposition came overwhelmingly from that country.

A sense of proportion is needed, of course. There was plenty of strong language used, both inside and outside the *aula*, about other decrees that were eventually approved. The large majorities in favor of the schema before the final stages surely indicate a good measure of support for the decree, not just weariness and the desire to get on with the next and more important item of business. Various journalists and writers defended *Inter Mirifica*. Walter Abbott, SJ, for example, editor of the conciliar decrees and assistant editor of *America* magazine, spoke in its defense at a dinner sponsored by *Motion Picture Industry* in early 1964—even while he permitted the different tones of Burke and Stuber in his edition. He argued that, while not entirely satisfactory, the decree nevertheless provided a "useful instrument" when understood in the spirit of the council and it witnessed to the Holy Spirit's guidance of the fathers. Another Jesuit, Enrico Baragli of the Italian periodical *Civiltà Cattolica*, provided a firm and reasoned defense of the decree in his book, *Inter Mirifica*, which is much the fullest study of the decree and its early reception.

The count of 503 who voted against the decree almost at the end (see above, p. 103) was paralleled by hostile votes on a number of other decrees. What is unusual about opposition to *Inter Mirifica* is that the votes against it mounted dramatically in the closing stages, whereas in the case of other contested decrees a text that was acceptable to the large majority—however begrudgingly so—was eventually found and the numbers voting against declined accordingly.

Another important factor, recognized by many at the time, was that if the council had extended the discussion, as a fair number of fathers wanted, then either the council itself would have been prolonged further, almost to breaking point, or various other decrees might have been curtailed or abandoned. *Gaudium et Spes*, whose survival was threatened in 1964, might have been a casualty. The mass media was already such a huge and complex topic that a small amount of extra time for debate probably would not have made much difference; to do justice to the subject, extended further debate looked necessary. In a sense, an improved *Inter Mirifica* was sacrificed for the greater good of the council as a whole.

SUBSEQUENT RECEPTION AND IMPLEMENTATION

The view that *Inter Mirifica* represented a missed opportunity—to compose something better on an extremely important subject—has prevailed since the council. Opinions differ, however, as to how serious the consequences have been. Some commentators have kept to the line voiced by the malcontents at the time of the council and have seen the increasing inability of the Catholic Church to influence the mass media as the sorry and inevitable result of the poverty of *Inter Mirifica*. Many of the later collections of essays on the council and its reception, some of which are included in Further Reading (see below, pp. 123–26), contain no articles on *Inter Mirifica* or only very slight treatment of it. The absence may be interpreted as a kind of embarrassed silence regarding the decree and its implementation.

An exception to this silence is to be found in Latourelle, *Vatican II*. The work, reflecting on the twenty-five years since the opening of the council, included articles by three Jesuits on *Inter Mirifica* and its reception: Avery (later Cardinal) Dulles, "Vatican II and Communications"; André Ruszkowski, " The Decree on the Means of Social Communication: Success or Failure of the Council?"; Robert White, "Mass Media and Culture in Contemporary Catholicism: The Significance of Vatican II." The articles survey the issues involved in the decree and its reception, with the second writer providing its most vigorous defense.

Ruszkowski drew a distinction. While he admitted that the decree was a "disappointment for those who would have wanted some in-depth doctrinal statements," he reckoned it fulfilled the expectations of those who had been involved in "the efforts that were already being made" and provided "authoritative encouragement to continue them within an institutional framework approved by the council." *Inter Mirifica*, he thought, "opened up a period of increasingly satisfactory initiatives and fulfillment on every level." He then went on to list the achievements that stemmed from the decree, directly or indirectly, as follows. The Pontifical Commission for Cinema, Radio and Television (see above, p. 93) was promoted by Pope Paul VI in 1964 into a full "Council" of the Roman curia, called the "Pontifical Council of Social Communications" (*Pontificium Consilium de Communicationibus Socialibus* = PCSC). Seven years later this Council published the pastoral instruction *Communio et Progressio*, in fulfillment of the mandate in the "Conclusions" of *Inter Mirifica*. The annual "World Day of Social Communications" was established. Numerous commissions were set up by episcopal conferences at national and regional levels in order to encourage Catholic participation in the mass media, in fulfillment of the directives of *Inter Mirifica*. Supporting the same conclusion, Robert White drew attention to the large number of Catholic radio stations that have sprung up since Vatican II at least partly in response to *Inter Mirifica*. There were, he said, at the time of writing, more than 350 such stations in Latin America alone.

Communio et Progressio is regarded by Jacob Srampickal, director of the Center for Social Communications at the Gregorian University, Rome, as "the *Magna Carta* of Christian communication with a positive, professional and concrete approach to communication and the

Church."[1] The document's first part, entitled "Christian View of Communication," provides a theological basis, which is rather lacking in *Inter Mirifica*. A second part treats of "The Contribution of the Media to Human Progress," and the third, "The Commitment of Catholics in the Media." Altogether the treatment is fuller and more theological than that of *Inter Mirifica*. The PCSC, in recent years under its energetic president, Archbishop John Foley, and secretary, Bishop Pierfranco Pastore, has issued a stream of other, shorter documents on particular issues relating to the media as well as a more general instruction, *Aetatis Novae*, in 1992, which was intended as a follow-up to *Communio et Progressio*. In these ways some of the limitations of *Inter Mirifica* have been overcome. But, of course, these Roman documents, though they have been translated into the main vernacular languages and have received some attention, possess less authority than *Inter Mirifica*, the decree of an ecumenical council, and much less diffusion than the latter, which is included in all the collections of conciliar decrees. Inevitably it is *Inter Mirifica*, with its limitations, that has remained at the forefront of attention outside specialist circles.

Another relevant consideration is that *Inter Mirifica* must be seen in the context of several other decrees of Vatican II that treat of communication. At the deepest and most theological level, *Dei Verbum* speaks of God's communication to us through the Word. A central concern of both *Gaudium et Spes* and *Ad Gentes* is the communication of the gospel message, in its richness and diversity, to Christians and to all people. *Unitatis Redintegratio* and *Nostra Aetate* treat more specifically of dialogue among Christians and with those of other faiths. All these decrees were important in the work of Vatican II. They contain some of the most innovative ideas of the council, and they are among the decrees that have gained the warmest "reception" subsequently. Altogether, therefore, the council gave much and fruitful attention to the overall theme of communication within which *Inter Mirifica* must be situated. This needs to be said even though there is obviously an element of special pleading. *Inter Mirifica* should be seen within this wider context, yet at the same time it must also be judged within the more specific dimension of communication—the mass media—that is its explicit and central concern.

PART IV

THE STATE OF THE QUESTIONS

Regarding the significance of *Inter Mirifica* for today, forty years after the end of the council, and for the future, thoughts may well be mixed.

On the one hand, disappointment with the quality of the document remains. During the council there eventually emerged quite widespread acknowledgment, both inside and outside the *aula*, that the decree had not measured up to expectations. There was, it is true, significant opposition, at various stages, to the contents of several other decrees: *Lumen Gentium*, *Dignitatis Humanae*, and *Unitatis Redintegratio* are clear examples. But the sense of disappointment and of inadequacy—rather than of opposition—was more pervasive for *Inter Mirifica* than for probably any other decree.

This sense of inadequacy, moreover, has remained. The mass media, the focus of the decree, have continued to grow in scale and influence. The world of Catholic media, to which the decree directed much of its attention, remains significant: in some places it has grown in importance, in others it has diminished. But far greater in scale is the secular media and here the influence of the Catholic Church seems marginal. Indeed, the media in much of the West—for long the heartland of the Catholic Church—are not slow to both marginalize and ridicule the church: anti-clerical and more specifically anti-Catholic slants are often evident. Catholics, and particularly Catholic teachings, are portrayed as narrow, backward looking, and divisive; serious discussion of religious issues is comparatively rare. This impotence might have been averted if a document had been promulgated of similar quality to *Gaudium et Spes* or *Dei Verbum* or *Unitatis Redintegratio:* one that gave a much fuller and sounder basis for thought and action.

Even within the world of Catholic media, differences among Catholics—dissent over *Humanae Vitae* was an early and glaring case (see above, pp. 73–74)—have prevented the unity of approach on moral and other issues that *Inter Mirifica* seeks and even presupposes. The document's firm emphasis upon clerical direction does not allow enough for the initiative and authority of the laity. The decree doesn't recognize sufficiently the reality of the situation even within the Catholic media, and has too little to say about the role of Catholics in the vast world of the media that lies beyond.

On the other hand, there is the document: a decree of an ecumenical council. The importance of the mass media is fully recognized in it and this is underlined by the fact that a whole decree is given to the issues. Would the result have been better if the media had featured in a chapter of *Gaudium et Spes*, one may ask? Maybe the treatment would have been better developed, given the extra two years of debate and reflection, yet the importance of the topic would have been highlighted less by a chapter than by a whole decree.

In a sense, too, awareness of the decree's limitations has stimulated further thought and action in a way that might not have occurred if a more polished document had emerged. There is a certain parallel with *Nostra Aetate*. The brevity, tentative nature, and limitations of the decree on the world's religions are evident. Yet it has opened doors and proved to be one of the most influential of all the council's decrees. Not that *Inter Mirifica* is tentative; rather, its critics would say it is too firm on some matters as well as unbalanced and incomplete. Yet the need to correct imperfections has likewise proved fruitful: by making clearer what was very guarded and implicit in the case of *Nostra Aetate*, through a more obvious rebalancing and wider coverage in the case of *Inter Mirifica*.

This rebalancing and wider coverage has come about partly through the series of documents issued by the PCSC, partly by the subsequent secondary literature on *Inter Mirifica*, and partly by the treatment of "communication" in other documents of Vatican II. In practice, the mass media have continued to develop with a speed that *Inter Mirifica* hinted at, to its credit, even if in ways that the council could not be expected to have foreseen. The birth and growth of the internet is the most dazzling development of which *Inter Mirifica* had no inkling. What further developments are in store for us? In this respect there is a parallelism with *Gaudium et Spes*, which did not foresee—as indeed it could not be expected to—the end of the Iron

Curtain or the political revival of Islam or various other events which have profoundly transformed the situation of the church in the world, the subject matter of the decree. But there is a difference, too. Whereas *Gaudium et Spes* provided a framework for future developments that has generally been well-received and indeed has continued to help the implementation of the decree, this is much less the case with *Inter Mirifica*. The latter seems to concentrate too much on a situation of church control over the media, a control that has largely vanished—if it ever existed—and to say too little that is relevant or helpful about the much larger world of secular media and of the responsibilities of Catholics within it. Altogether there is much more of a sense of addressing the real world in *Gaudium et Spes* than in *Inter Mirifica*.

Nevertheless *Inter Mirifica* merits re-reading today. We can be grateful that the council, which appears set to guide the Christian community into the foreseeable future, produced a full decree on the mass media. It shows the church is ready to face the most pressing challenges of the day; the Incarnation means that Christians cannot escape from the world in which they live. The decree reminds us of the wonders and benefits of recent inventions in the mass media as well as of the dangers inherent in them. Everyone has a personal responsibility in these areas of life: we cannot shelter behind the works of others. The decree reminds us of the subtle and often hidden pressures of the media, that we need to tune our ears and eyes. There are, too, the particular opportunities and responsibilities of those engaged professionally in the media. Regarding media more closely linked to the Catholic Church, the latter has a right to possess and use these means in order to spread the gospel message and, more generally, to build up the body of Christ. In all this there will be struggle—to discern the best ways forward and to put them into practice—as well as fruits. The media are an image of the work of our redemption.

NOTES

1. The head (prefect) and number two (secretary) of the commission/ secretariat were usually the prefect and secretary of the corresponding department (dicastery/congregation) of the Roman Curia; many members of the commissions were officials of the dicasteries, the others being bishops and theologians (called *periti*) from around the world; and the meetings took place in Rome, often in the office of the relevant dicastery.

2. *ADA*, passim, for the *vota*. For the schemata: *Schemata Constitutionum et Decretorum*, 4 series (Vatican City: Typis Polyglottis Vaticanis, 1962–63).

3. There is no doubt, in my mind, about the fundamental divide that emerged in the council between the so-called conservative or traditionalist minority and the liberal or progressive majority, even though there were, of course, many nuances within the overall picture. The labels "conservative," "traditionalist," "liberal," and "progressive" may seem inappropriate and were indeed disputed and/or disowned by many at the time. Liberals might claim to be the true conservatives, arguing that the so-called conservatives or traditionalists were rather "moderns" living in a relatively recent time-warp, dating from the nineteenth century and the dominance of ultramontanism in the church. Vice versa, conservatives might claim that it was they who were bringing true freedom and progress to the church, in contrast to the enslavement to the world that resulted from liberalism.

It is to avoid these dubious labels, while recognizing the divide, for the sake of convenience and at the cost of a certain over-simplification, that I am calling the "conservative" minority A (members of this minority = A's) and the "progressive" minority B (members of this minority = B's). The divide showed up early and sharply in the debates on the sources of revelation and on the church that eventually resulted in the constitutions *Dei Verbum* and *Lumen Gentium*. It surfaced, in various forms and with varying nuances, in the debates on most other decrees, including *Gaudium et Spes*.

119

4. *ADA*, II/5 (Africa), pp. 537–39.

5. Alberigo, *Vatican II*, i, pp. 97–135, and Turbanti, *GS*, pp. 32–48, provide useful summaries of the *vota*.

6. The (full) members of the council were, essentially, all the bishops in the church, plus a relatively few others, such as some cardinals who were not bishops and some heads of religious orders. These full members were called "fathers" (Latin, *patres*) of the council. Distinct from them, with many important roles but without full membership and therefore without the rights to speak and vote in the debates, were the theologians/*periti* (see above, p. 119, note 1), "observers" (especially important were those representing other Christian churches), journalists, and many other individuals contributing to the organization and running of the council.

7. In the first week of the council in October 1962, the preparatory commissions and secretariats had been transformed into ten "conciliar commissions," each one of the latter usually keeping the name of the corresponding preparatory commission. Initially, two-thirds of the members of these new commissions were elected by the fathers of the council and one-third were appointed by Pope John XXIII; subsequently the commissions grew in size considerably through fresh appointments.

8. For much of the material in this sub-section, including the quotations, and the references for these quotations, see pp. 270-331 of my chapter 5, "The Church in the World (*Ecclesia ad Extra*)," in vol. 4 of Alberigo, *Vatican II*.

9. See, Alberigo, *Vatican II*, iv, pp. 282–86.

10. See p. 123.

11. Latourelle, *Vatican II*, iii, p. 451.

12. Alberigo, *Vatican II*, iv, pp. 377–81.

13. Marcel Lefèbvre (1905–91) attended Vatican II as superior general of the Holy Ghost Congregation and (titular) archbishop of Synnada in Phrygia. An outspoken leader of the conservative minority at the council, he resigned as superior general in 1968 and founded the Society of Saint Pius X as a traditionalist community, opposed to many of the reforms of Vatican II. He was suspended from his episcopal functions (*a divinis*) in 1976 and was excommunicated in 1988 along with the four bishops whom he ordained to continue the community.

14. Figures kindly supplied by Pierpaolo Finaldi, commissioning editor of CTS.

15. Alberigo, *Vatican II*.

16. For a convenient conspectus of the theological aspects, including the critiques mentioned below, and references to further literature, see Latourelle, *Vatican II*: chapter 37, Luis Ladaria, "Humanity in the Light of

Christ in the Second Vatican Council"; chapter 38, Luigi M. Rulla, Franco Imoda, and Joyce Ridick, "Anthropology of the Christian Vocation: Conciliar and Postconciliar Aspects"; chapter 39, Edouard Hamel, "The Foundations of Human Rights in Biblical Theology following the Orientations of *Gaudium et spes.*" For subsequent literature, see the works under Aparicio Valls (1997), Bordeyne (2004), and Urribari (2005) in Further Reading (below, p. 126).

17. Latourelle, *Vatican II*, ii, pp. 460–61.

18. Latourelle, *Vatican II*, ii, p. 396.

19. Latourelle, *Vatican II*, ii, p. 419.

20. See Hervé Carrier, "The Contribution of the Church to Culture," in Latourelle, *Vatican II*, iii, p. 460.

21. Article in the French newspaper *Le Figaro*, as reported in *The Tablet*, 21 August 2004, p. 3.

22. Alfred T. Hennelly, ed., *Liberation Theology: A Documentary History* (Maryknoll, NY: Orbis Books, 1990), p. 40.

23. Ibid., pp. 403 and 461–506. Other relevant papal statements and those of the Congregation are conveniently given in English translation in Parts 5 and 6 of the same work.

24. Isaiah 42:1–4; 49:1–6; 50:4–9; 52:13—53:12.

SECTION II

DECREE ON MEANS OF SOCIAL COMMUNICATION: *INTER MIRIFICA*

1. Jacob Srampickal and Leela Joseph, *Babel to Babri Masjid and Beyond: Pastoral Communication and Media Involvement in the Indian Catholic Church* (Delhi: Media House, 2003), p. 34.

PART V
FURTHER READING

THE STORY AT VATICAN II

The story of how *Gaudium et Spes* and *Inter Mirifica* emerged through the preparation and years of the council is told in detail in the recently published *History of Vatican II*, ed. Giuseppe Alberigo and Joseph Komonchak (Maryknoll, NY: Orbis/Leuven: Peeters, 1995–), 4 vols. so far, with the fifth (and last) volume forthcoming.

The full texts (in Latin) of the speeches in the *aula*, the written submissions, and the various drafts of the two decrees, are found in: *Acta Synodalia Sacrosancti Concilii Oecumenici Vaticani II*, 4 vols. (Vatican City: Typis Polyglottis Vaticanis, 1970–80).

The debates in the *aula* were summarized at the time in lively form by the Redemptorist priest Francis Xavier Murphy, who wrote under the pseudonym "Xavier Rynne" (Rynne was his mother's maiden name)—thus circumventing the council's rules of secrecy—and published his weekly reports in *The New Yorker*. He attended the council as a journalist and had wide contacts. At the end of each session of the council, an expanded version of his reports was published (still under the name of Xavier Rynne) in book form, ultimately in four volumes with the following titles: *Letters from Vatican City...First Session* (1963); *The Second Session* (1964); *The Third Session* (1965); *The Fourth Session* (1966), all published by Faber and Faber of London and New York: reprinted by Orbis Books in 1999. The volumes represent the fullest and most accessible contemporary account of the debates in English.

Yves Congar, *Mon journal du concile*, 2 vols. (Paris: Cerf, 2002), is without equal as the frank and fascinating account of a Dominican theologian who played a very active and influential role at the council. It contains much material relevant to *Gaudium et Spes*.

The United States's contribution to the debates, including the texts of the bishops' speeches in English translation, is conveniently covered in

American Participation in the Second Vatican Council, ed. Vincent A. Yzermans (New York: Sheed and Ward, 1967), chapters 4 and 5.

The fullest account of the evolution of *Gaudium et Spes* during the council is Giovanni Turbanti's *Un concilio per il mondo moderno: La redazione della constituzione pastorale "Gaudium et spes" del Vaticano II* (Bologna: Il Mulino, 2001).

The fullest account of the passage of *Inter Mirifica* through the council is Ernesto Baragli's *Inter Mirifica: Introduzione, Storia, Discussione, Commento, Documentazione* (Rome: Pontificia Università Gregoriana, 1969).

The roles of the two popes in the council are treated in the biographies by Peter Hebblethwaite: *John XXIII, Pope of the Council* (London: Chapman,1984) and *Paul VI: The First Modern Pope* (New York/Mahwah, NJ: Paulist Press, 1993).

TEXTS AND COMMENTARIES

The texts of *Gaudium et Spes* and *Inter Mirifica* in English translation, together with some introduction and commentary, are conveniently found in two popular paperback collections of all the decrees of Vatican II: Walter Abbott, ed., *The Documents of Vatican II* (New York: America Press/London: Chapman, 1966 and numerous reprints); and Austin Flannery, ed., *Vatican Council II: The Conciliar and Post Conciliar Documents* (Dublin: Dominican Publications/Northport: Costello Publishing, 1975 and reprints).

Decrees of the Ecumenical Councils, ed. Norman Tanner (London: Sheed and Ward, subsequently Continuum/Georgetown: Georgetown University Press, 1990), vol. 2, pp. 843–49 and 1069–1135, contains the Latin original of *Inter Mirifica* and *Gaudium et Spes* together with a facing English translation. The subject index (vol. 2, pp. 1239–1342) allows readers to follow issues in *Inter Mirifica* and *Gaudium et Spes* through the earlier ecumenical councils.

An invaluable recent work for the scholar of the text of *Gaudium et Spes* is *Constitutio Pastoralis de Ecclesia in Mundo Huius Temporis: Gaudium et Spes,* ed. Francisco Gil Hellín (Vatican City: Libreria Editrice Vaticana, 2003). The work sets side by side, in the original Latin, the four principal versions through which the text passed during the course of the council. It contains other useful background material.

The best commentary on *Gaudium et Spes* in English remains that in *Commentary on the Documents of Vatican II,* ed. Herbert Vorgrimler (London and New York: Burns & Oates, 1967–69), vol. 5. The volume includes a useful history of the evolution of the decree. *Inter Mirifica* is covered briefly in vol. 1, pp. 89–104.

RECEPTION AND IMPLEMENTATION

For the reception and development of *Inter Mirifica* and *Gaudium et Spes* in the magisterium, principally papal, see the encyclicals and other documents mentioned on pp. 64–65 and 114–15. English translations of most of them are found in *The Papal Encyclicals*, ed. Claudia Carlen (Ann Arbor: Pierian Press, 1990), vol. 5 (1958–1981); *The Encyclicals of John Paul II*, ed. J. Michael Miller (Huntington: Our Sunday Visitor, 1996); *Vatican Council II*, vol. 1, *The Conciliar and Post Conciliar Documents*, and vol. 2, *More Postconciliar Documents*, ed. Austin Flannery (Northport: Costello Publishing, 1996–98); *Church and Social Communications: Basic Documents*, ed. Franz-Joseph Eilers (Manila: Logos, 1993, 1997); *Catechism of the Catholic Church* (Vatican City, Libreria Editrice Vaticana, 1994).

For the early reception of *Inter Mirifica*, see the work by Baragli, *Inter Mirifica* (see p. 124).

The only recent full-length book (known to me) that focuses exclusively on the reception of *Gaudium et Spes* is Vincenzo De Cicco and A. Scarano's *La Chiesa nel mondo contemporaneo. La recezione della Gaudium et spes* (Naples: Chirico, 2003).

For the influence of *Gaudium et Spes* upon liberation theology, see *Liberation Theology: A Documentary History*, ed. Alfred T. Hennelly (Maryknoll, NY: Orbis Books, 1990).

For the general topic of reception, see especially *The Jurist* 57 (1997), no. 1, reprinted as *Reception and Communion among Churches*, ed. Hervé Legrand, Julio Manzanares and Antonio García y García (Washington, DC: Catholic University of America Press, 1997).

Of many other studies that treat of *Gaudium et Spes* and/or *Inter Mirifica*, and their reception and implementation, the following are especially noteworthy, in chronological order of publication and with emphasis upon those published in English:

Studia Moralia, 4 (1966): the issue was devoted to *Gaudium et Spes* and contains a valuable and early collection of articles on the decree.
J. H. Miller, ed., *Vatican II: An Interfaith Appraisal* (Notre Dame: Association Press, 1966).
Adrian Hastings, *A Concise Guide to the Documents of the Second Vatican Council* (London: Darton, Longmann & Todd, 1968–69).
Joseph Gremillion, ed., *The Gospel of Peace and Justice: Catholic Social Teaching since Pope John* (Maryknoll, NY: Orbis Books, 1976).
Rodger Charles, *The Social Teaching of Vatican II: Its Origin and Development* (Oxford: Plater Publications, 1982).

Gerald M. Fagin, ed., *Vatican II: Open Questions and New Horizons* (Wilmington: Glazier, 1984).

Alberic Stacpoole, ed., *Vatican II: By Those Who Were There* (London: Chapman, 1986).

Timothy E. O'Connell, ed., *Vatican II and Its Documents: An American Reappraisal* (Wilmington: Glazier, 1986).

Giuseppe Alberigo, Jean-Pierre Jossua, and Joseph A. Komonchak, eds., *The Reception of Vatican II* (Washington, DC: Catholic University of America Press, 1987).

Lucien Richard, Daniel Harrington, and John W. O'Malley, eds., *Vatican II: The Unfinished Agenda: A Look to the Future* (New York/Mahwah, NJ: Paulist Press, 1987).

John Mahoney, *The Making of Moral Theology: A Study of the Roman Catholic Tradition* (Oxford: Clarendon Press, 1987).

René Latourelle, ed., *Vatican II: Assessment and Perspectives Twenty-Five Years After (1962–1987)*, 3 vols. (New York/Mahwah, NJ: Paulist Press, 1988–89).

Maria Carmen Aparicio Valls, *La plenitud del Ser Humano en Cristo: la revelación en la "Gaudium et Spes"* (Rome: Editrice Pontificia Università Gregoriana, 1997).

Anthony J. Cernera, ed., *Vatican II: The Continuing Agenda* (Fairfield: Sacred Heart University Press, 1997).

Gilles Routhier, ed., *Vatican II au Canada: enracinement et réception* (Québec: Fides, 2001).

Maureen Sullivan, *101 Questions and Answers on Vatican II* (New York/Mahwah, NJ: Paulist Press, 2002).

William Madges and Michael J. Daley, eds., *Vatican II: Forty Personal Stories* (Mystic: Twenty-Third Publications, 2003).

Jacob Srampickal and Leela Joseph, *Babel to Babri Masjid and Beyond: Pastoral Communication and Media Involvement in the Indian Catholic Church* (Delhi: Media House, 2003).

Austen Ivereigh, ed., *Unfinished Journey: The Church 40 Years after Vatican II: Essays for John Wilkins* (New York: Continuum, 2003).

Philippe Bordeyne, *L'homme et son angoisse: La théologie morale de "Gaudium et spes"* (Paris: Cerf, 2004).

Gabino Uribarri, ed., *Teología y Nueva Evangelización*, articles by Angel Cordovilla and Santiago Madrigal (Bilbao: Desclée, forthcoming 2005).

INDEX

Abbott, Walter, 64, 110
Ad Gentes, ix, 74
Adnexa, 33, 51, 53, 58
Aetatis Novae, 115
Agagianian, Gregory, 29, 103
Alberigo, Giuseppe, 65
Alfrink, Bernard, 27, 102
America, 112
Andrew, Agnellus, 94
Anglican Church, 88; *see also*
    Williams, Rowan
apartheid, 4
Apostolicam Actuositatem, ix, 115
Arrupe, Pedro, 34–35
Association Press, New York, 111
Athaide, Dominic, 20

Baptist World Alliance, 111
Baragli, Enrico, 113
Bea, Augustin, 13, 98
Beck, George, 28, 97, 98, 100
Bellosillo, Pilar, 28
Benedict XV, Pope, 84
Benedict XVI, Pope; *see* Ratzinger,
    Joseph
Benítez Avalos, Felipe, 25
birth control, 15, 21, 22, 31, 52
Blair, Tony, 85
Blajot, Jorge, 32
Bologna circle, 31
British Broadcasting Corporation
    (BBC), 94
Buddhists, 74
Burke, Thomas, 110–11

Calvin, John, 70
Cantero Cuadrado, Pedro, 98
Caprile, Giovanni, 31
Casti Connubii, 51
Catechism of the Catholic Church, 64, 73
Catholic Reporter, 102
Catholic Truth Society, 64
Centesimus Annus, 65
Cento, Fernando, 13, 96–97
Christus Dominus, ix
Civardi, Luigi, 99
CM, *see* Mixed Commission
Coderre, Gérard, 20
Cogley, John, 102
Commission for the Lay Apostolate,
    the Press and the Moderation of
    Shows, 96–97
Commission of the Lay Apostolate,
    x, xii, 5, 7–8, 96, 99–100, 102
Commonweal, 102
Communio et Progressio, 114–15
Communism, 4, 10, 15, 27, 34, 37, 46,
    55, 69, 70, 81; *see also* Marx, Karl
Comunione e Liberazione, 83
Congar, Yves, 9, 30
Congregation of the Doctrine of the
    Faith, 77, 79; *see also* Holy Office;
    Ratzinger, Joseph
Copin, Noël, 30
Cuban missile crisis, 8, 27, 58
Čule, Peter, 18

Daniélou, Jean, 102
Darmajuwana, Justinus, 16

D'Avach, Joseph, 98
Dearden, John, 21
De Castro Mayer, Antonio, 99
De Ecclesia, 11, 18; *see also Lumen Gentium*
Dei Verbum, ix, xi, 35, 62–64, 115–16, 119 note 3
De la Chanonie, Pierre, 20
De la Salle, John, 17
De Llanos, José Maria, 32
De Proença Sigaud, Gerald, 34–35
De Provenchères, Charles, 23
Deskur, Andrzej, 94
Dignitatis Humanae, ix, 46, 63, 111, 116
Doctrinal Commission, x, xii, 5, 7–8, 11
Documentation Catholique, La, 30
Döpfner, Julius, 13, 29, 103
D'Souza, Eugene, 99
Dulles, Avery, 114
Duval, Léon-Etienne, 98

Echo der Zeit, 31
Economist, The, 26
Etchegaray, Roger, 11
European Union, 77
Evangelium Vitae, 65

Falkland Islands, war, 85
Fédération Internationale de la Jeunesse Catholique, 28
Felici, Pericles, 11, 26, 33, 102
Feltin, Maurice, 27
Fesquet, Henri, 30, 102, 112
Flannery, Austin, 64
Flynn, Timothy, 94
Focolarini, 83
Foley, John, 115
Francis de Sales, 17
Franco, Francisco, 31
Frankfurter Allgemeine Zeitung, 31
French revolution (1789), 55
Frings, Joseph, 18, 102

Galileo, 49
Gandhi, Mahatma, 20
Garcia de Sierra y Mendez, Secundus, 17
Gaudium et Spes, ix–xii, 1–90 passim, 111, 113, 115–26
Gerlier, Pierre, 102
Ghave, Vinobba, 20
globalization, 47, 70, 80
Godfrey, William, 98
Golland Trindade, Henrique, 18
Gonzalez Martin, Marcel, 98
Gravissimum Educationis, ix
Gregorian University, Rome, 65, 114
Gregory XVI, Pope, 46, 56
Guano, Aemilius, 21, 28–29
Gulf War I, 85
Gulf War II, 85

Hamel, Edouard, 65
Hannan, Philip, 27, 28
Häring, Bernard, 15, 31, 102
Harper's, 102
Haubtmann, Pierre, 32
Heenan, John, 13, 15
Hengsbach, Franz, 27
Hermaniuk, Maximus, 34
Hindus, 74
Höffner, Joseph, 98
Holy Land, 84
Holy Office, 5, 21; *see also* Congregation of the Doctrine of the Faith
Humanae Salutis, 3
Humanae Vitae, 21, 73–74, 116–17
Hurley, Denis, 4

Ignatius of Loyola, 17
Imoda, Franco, 68
Index Librorum Prohibitorum, 95–96
Industrial Revolution, 55
Informations Catholiques Internationales, 30
Inter Mirifica, ix, xi–xii, 93–118 passim, 121, 123–26

International Catholic Migration Commission, 25
Iron Curtain, 69, 80–81, 117–18
Islam, 82, 118; *see also* Muslims
Italian Commission for Films, 99

Jews, 74, 89
John XXIII, Pope, 3–6, 8, 10, 11, 15, 25, 36, 41, 47, 55, 58, 62–63, 84, 93, 98, 111, 120 note 7
John Paul II, Pope, 64–65, 73, 77, 79, 81, 85, 88; *see also* Wojtyła, Karol

Kaiser, Robert, 102
Kathpress, 31
Keegan, Patrick, 25
Kennedy, John, 20, 27
King, Martin Luther, 20
KIPA, 31
Klepacz, Michal, 18
KNA, 31
Kowalski, Zygfryd, 18
Küng, Hans, 31

Laborem Exercens, 65
La Civiltà Cattolica, 31, 75, 113
La Croix, 30, 102
Ladaria, Luis, 65
Lándazuri Ricketts, Juan,14, 16
Latourelle, René, 65, 114
La Valle, Raniero, 31
L'Avvenire d'Italia, 31
League of Nations, 84
Lefèbvre, Joseph, 102
Lefèbvre, Marcel, 61, 120 note 13
Léger, Paul, 15–16, 22, 98
Legionaries of Christ, 83
Le Monde, 30, 102
Leo XIII, Pope, 6, 15, 47, 55, 62, 77
Lepanto, battle of, 84
Lercaro, Giacomo, 24, 29, 31, 103
liberation theology, 78–79
Liénart, Achilles, 13–14
L'Institut Catholique (Paris), 32

Lokuang, Stanislaus, 24
L'Osservatore Romano, 31
Lourdusamy, Duraisamy, 20
Lumen Gentium, ix, xi, 8, 29, 35, 41, 49, 63–65, 74, 106, 111, 116, 119 note 3; *see also* De Ecclesia
Luther, Martin, 70

Malines text, 7–8, 10
Malula, Joseph, 20
Marty, François,18
Marx, Karl, 15, 55, 79, 81; *see also* Communism
Mater et Magistra, 6, 8, 10, 25, 47, 55
Maximus IV Saigh, 19, 28
Medellín, 78
Mejia, Jorge, 102
Ménager, Jacques, 98
Meouchi, Paul, 14
Methodists; *see* World Methodist Council
Miranda Prorsus, 93, 95
Mirari Vos, 46, 56
Mixed Commission (CM), x, 7–10, 12–13, 15, 21–22, 29, 32–33, 36–37
Morcillo, Casimir, 14
Muelder, Walter, 30
Murphy, Francis Xavier; *see* Rynne, Francis Xavier
Murray, John Courtney, 102
Muslims, 74, 77, 82, 84–85, 87; *see also* Islam

National Catholic Welfare Conference, 31
Neo-catechumenate, 83
Newman, John Henry, 15
New Republic, 102
New Yorker, The, 30–31
Nicaea I, council, 70
Nicolau, Miguel, 32
Nkongolo, Joseph, 22
Norris, John, 25, 26, 28

North American College, Rome, 94
Nostra Aetate, ix, 62–63, 104, 115, 117
Novak, Michael, 102
Ntuyahaga, Michel, 27
nuclear weapons, 8, 27–28, 31, 35,
    58–59, 86

O'Connor, Martin, 94, 97
Optatam Totius, ix, 62
Opus Dei, 83
Orientalium Ecclesiarum, ix
Orthodox Church, 88
Ottaviani, Alfredo, 5, 21–22

Pacem in Terris, 8, 10, 27, 41, 47,
    58–59, 84
pacifism, 58–59
Pastore, Pierfranco, 115
Paul IV, Pope, 96
Paul VI, Pope, xi, 8, 11, 15, 21, 24,
    35, 37, 47, 52, 58, 61, 65, 73, 76,
    84–85, 96, 103, 114
Pavan, Pietro, 10
Perfectae Caritatis, ix
Perraudin, André, 99
Philips, Gérard, 9
Pilot, 102
Pius IX, Pope, 56
Pius X, Pope, 120 note 13
Pius XI, Pope, 15, 22, 51, 98
Pius XII, Pope, 15, 22, 51, 84, 93–95,
    98, 111
Pontifical Council for Cinema, Radio
    and Television, 93, 108
Pontifical Council of Culture, 77
Pontifical Council of Social Commu-
    nication, x, 114–15, 117
Populorum Progressio, 65
Presbyterorum Ordinis, ix
Prou, Jean, 17

Rahner, Karl, 9, 33–34
Ratzinger, Joseph, 77, 79

Razón y Fe, 31
Redemptoris Hominum, 65
Reetz, Benedict, 99
Rerum Novarum, 6, 47, 55
Ridick, 68
Romero Menjibar, Felix, 17
Ruffini, Ernesto, 15, 21–22
Rugambwa, Laurean, 26
Rulla, Luigi, 68
Rupp, Jean, 26–27
Russian Revolution (1917), 55
Ruszkowski, André, 114
Rynne, Francis Xavier, 30

Sacrosanctum Concilium, ix, xi, 35,
    62–64, 100
Sana, 97
Scheele, Paul-Werner, 31
Schema XIII / XVII, *see Gaudium et
    Spes*
Schmitt, Paul, 17
Secretariat for Christian Unity,
    13–14
Secretariat for the Press and the
    Moderation of Shows, x, 93–94,
    96–97
Secretariat of State, 108
Šeper, Franjo, 26
Sheehan, John, 15
signs of the times, 9, 14–17, 25, 30, 41
Silva Henriquez, Raúl, 16
Soares de Resende, Sebastian, 16
Soegijapranata, Albert, 98
Sollicitudo Rei Socialis, 65
Spanish Civil War, 84
Spellman, Francis, 13
Srampickal, Jacob, 114
Staverman, Rudolf, 22
Stourm, René, 96–97, 100–101
Stuber, Stanley, 111
Suenens, Leo, 7, 16, 29, 103
Swiss Guards, 102
Syllabus of Errors (1864), 56

Synod of Bishops (1974), 76
Synod of Bishops (1977), 76

Tchidimbo, Raymond, 16
Tenhumbert, Heinrich, 17
Thomas Aquinas, 56
Time, 102
Trent, council of, 9, 43–45, 70

Unità, 31
Unitatis Redintegratio, ix, 62–63, 88, 115–16
United Nations, 27, 58–59, 84

Vairo, Giuseppe, 15
Vajta, Vilmos, 30
Vasquez, Juan, 28–29
Vatican I, council, 9, 43, 49
Vatican Radio, 98
Veritatis Splendor, 65, 73
Vincent de Paul, 17
Vischer, Lukas, 30
Vorgrimler, Herbert, 64
Votum on marriage, x, 51

Ward, Barbara, 25
Ward, Mary, 17
Weigel, Gustave, 111
Wenger, Antoine, 30, 102, 112
White, Robert, 114
Williams, Rowan, 85
Wojtyła, Karol, 10, 14, 32, 81; *see also* John Paul II
World Council of Churches, 30
World Day of Social Communications, 114
World Methodist Council, 30
World Union of Catholic Women's Organizations, 28–29
World War I, 58, 84
World War II, 58, 84

Yago, Bernard, 23
Yü Pin, Paul, 15

Zarranz y Pueyo, Juan, 98–99
Ziadé, Ignatius, 17
Zoa, Jean-Baptiste, 24
Zoungrana, Paul, 25